Canting Arms

CANTING ARMS

EMILIAN GALAICU-PĂUN

TRANSLATED BY ADAM J. SORKIN

AND DIANA MANOLE, LIDIA VIANU,

CLAUDIA SEREA, RAREȘA GALAICU, CRISTINA CÎRSTEA DANILOV, STEFANIA HIRTOPANU

PHONEME MEDIA | DEEP VELLUM

DALLAS, TEXAS

Phoneme Media, an imprint of Deep Vellum Publishing
3000 Commerce St., Dallas, Texas 75226
deepvellum.org · @deepvellum

Deep Vellum is a 501c3 nonprofit literary arts organization founded in 2013 with the mission to bring the world into conversation through literature.

Support for this publication has been provided in part by the National Endowment for the Arts, the Texas Commission on the Arts, the City of Dallas Office of Arts and Culture, and the George and Fay Young Foundation.

Paperback ISBN: 978-1-64605-274-5 | ebook ISBN 978-1-64605-295-0

LIBRARY OF CONGRESS CONTROL NUMBER: 2023037927

Cover design by Lexi Earle
Interior layout and typesetting by KGT
PRINTED IN CANADA

CONTENTS

(Diaphragm)

II. *Seven Poems*

Acknowledgments

The translators express thanks to the editors of the following publications, in which some of the poems in this book appeared earlier: the literary journals *Absinthe*, *Orient Express*, *3:AM Magazine*, *Connotation Press*, *Asymptote*, *Poem*, and *Poetry London* and the books *Singular Destinies: Contemporary Poets of Bessarabia*, ed. Adam J. Sorkin, Cristina Cîrstea, and Sean Cotter (Editura Cartier, 2003); *A Fine Line: New Poetry from Eastern and Central Europe*, ed. Jean Boase-Beier, Alexandra Büchler, and Fiona Sampson (Arc Publications, 2004); *Born in Utopia: An Anthology of Modern and Contemporary Romanian Poetry*, ed. Carmen Firan and Paul Doru Mugur with Edward Foster (Talisman House, 2006); and *The Vanishing Point That Whistles: An Anthology of Contemporary Romanian Poetry*, ed. Paul Doru Mugur with Adam J. Sorkin and Claudia Serea (Talisman House, 2011).

Thanks also to the judges of the 2017–18 John Dryden Translation Competition, sponsored by the British Comparative Literature Association and the British Centre for Literary Translation at the University of East Anglia, who awarded second prize to selections from this book. Those poems were published in *Comparative Critical Studies*, the journal of the British Comparative Literature Association (Edinburgh University Press).

Adam J. Sorkin acknowledges the support of the University College of the Pennsylvania State University and Penn State Brandywine.

He also thanks Dorin Tudoran, Aura Maru, and Vasile Gribincea who read this manuscript at the poet's request and offered their comments and/or suggestions.

Finally, warmest gratitude to Emilian Galaicu-Păun for his unflagging encouragement and patience.

Introduction

According to the legend recounted by Dimitrie Cantemir, a notable ruler, scholar, states-man, composer, and poet, the fourteenth-century Prince Dragoș was hunting when his dog, Molda, exhausted by the chase, drowned in the river. The dog's name, given to the river, became the name of the country of Moldova.

Along with the country's name, this early Enlightenment prince is credited with bring-ing winemaking to the region, where it has been one of the main industries for over five hun-dred years. Indeed, if you find yourself in Chișinău, Moldova, dear reader, I hope it will be on the weekend when National Wine Day takes place and the city is full of parades celebrat-ing the harvest and the country's history of winemaking.

This city of wine cellars and limestone buildings, churches and Soviet-style apartment blocks is the hometown of poet Emilian Galaicu-Păun.

I begin this introduction with a historical reference and a place name because even though his work travels through a multitude of cultures, it always comes back to the words of his native language. The metaphysics of this poet, escaping from the language spoken in the streets of his native city, always returns to it.

The multiplicity of references to cultures and heritages, the multivocal perspective so apparent in this work, also has its root in the city's location on the borderland of various empires, from once powerful Hungarian and Polish kingdoms to Ottoman, Russian, Soviet, and Romanian spheres of influence. The city has been the center of multicultural histo-ries and tragic silences, too: once nearly half Jewish, it has been nearly emptied of its Jews. Still, it is a place where over the years many languages have echoed: Yiddish and Turkish, Hungarian and Romanian, Ukrainian, Russian, and Gagauzian were all spoken here.

I insist on mentioning this history not because the book in your hands has to do with historical narratives of empires, but because it is a product of their clash. The book you are holding right now comes from a place that is a crossroads between East and West, a place of rich and diverse history, yes, but also linguistic possibility, a place where translation and intercultural conversation are organic. Thus it is not at all surprising to find out that this book's author is someone who studied in one cultural sphere (USSR's Gorky Institute in Moscow) but lives in a very different cultural sphere (that of the Moldovan language, which is by all accounts really a Romanian language that traveled from Moldova to Romania and back—not unlike the spirit of Mihai Eminescu, the late Romantic poet who is considered the national bard in both countries). Meanwhile, his intricate and nuanced poetic landscape is in conversation with a very different sphere of poetic influence, namely, the works of French author Ronald Barthes and his seductive ideas of the pleasures of/and of the text itself.

As you turn the pages and meet poems rich in irony and historical and cultural allusions, know that they aren't there because the author is trying to be a "difficult" or fancy academic poet as some critics might imply, but very much because his work mirrors a non-normative historical and cultural circumstance, a crossroads.

•

Let me begin with what I find most impressive: how direct this poet's metaphysics seems to be as he addresses us through this vast and intricate landscape:

> "just to keep you current: I'm the one who plugs
> two fingers in the socket and through the
> electrical circuit stretches my hand deep into the night
> feeling my way to you . . ."

This metaphysics isn't simple or plain, but it also isn't obtuse. It is filled with a political charge and with an irony that keeps the charge alive even after the context of the particular situation that gave rise to the poem's occasion might be over. At times there is a flavor of lyric fabulism to his vision of history:

"in a

small country stained everywhere with ink, what kind of ink would
you have for your small country? red! god
inscribes the dead in black ink, and the living in red.
the mothers left the east going west,
each carrying a bundle with brains."

Yet as soon as you think you might be reading an example of an exotic East European voice, you see a direct echo of the Western voice reflected right back to you, reader:

"I have made my

boots out of blackest soil. now I could exclaim (thirty-three
years after Sylvia Plath): motherland,
black shoe in which I have lived like a foot
having learned to walk to the cadence of a foreign language. I can't
even say which foot is which."

Here it is, our American/West European cultural empire gazing back at us from the mirror a Romanian poet puts before us. Few Americans may know who Romania's national poets are, but here it's Sylvia Plath who looks back at us from the large and intricate panorama of voices and influences that form this poet's work. Here she is, along with many other voices, as we overhear the echo from the so-called borderland of the West, where we find "the pig asleep with its masters on the straw mattress as big as / a country . . . " No, the complexity here isn't because the author is trying to be fancy. The complexity here is because our world is large and contains multitudes. On one page you might find an echo of Plath, on another Pavese, on yet another Trakl. What is fascinating is how organic it all is, this mix of influences, how it all fits together in the world of this poet, where "unruly alphabets grow between the thighs of girls . . . " Yes, Emilian Galaicu-Păun's historical circumstance is, quite often, charged with eros:

"following her, I remembered only her going by. Her walk, as if she wore an almost ripe

pomegranate (in Romanian, *rodie*, in French, *grenade*) between her thighs . . .
you could hear her blood pulsing at her
wrists like a bracelet
of hot rubies—all that's remained after a revolution, two wars . . . "

This eros isn't a mere isolated incident, but one that happens in the context of half a dozen other emotions, historical events, and metaphysical inquiries. The poet clashes categories and mythologies against one another, here "*cainabel*" is one word, Galaicu-Păun's "evangelist writes through revelation . . . "

"Things fall apart, the center cannot hold," Yeats once told us. But what happens after? What happens if language isn't there merely to deliver information, when a poem isn't *about* an event, but is an event in *itself*? Which is to say, when a poet's language isn't telling us a neat story but instead the poet admits, "I swallow a letter until it sticks in my throat . . . " What then?

What happens when translated into our English—that is to say, the language of empire, the poet attests: "a poem is—exactly the same as an empire." What then?

"to recite
poems in prison, ion mureşan points out, is the equivalent of organizing
a mass escape."

What happens if the truth isn't in the message, but in the desire to deliver one? "I said everything" the poet admits, and adds right away, "I didn't say anything." Yet the word is out. This is a word.

Welcome to the world of Emilian Galaicu-Păun, dear readers. I hope you enjoy the ride. I know I did.

—Ilya Kaminsky

I. *Selected Poems*

Ascension

heavy as honey, from the ladle of his overturned nimbus
the flesh of his body slowly seeps
deep inside him through the sieve
of his blood: it trickles downward
over his face, molds itself to his chin, his neck,
his rounded shoulders, then flows along
his arms to his fists until it reaches the tips
of his fingers and his hands unclench into
finger-candles. for sacred as
holy oil from the ladle of his nimbus
the flesh of his body spills away,
anoints his chest, his abdomen,
bifurcates, letting the lotus of his virility
unfurl in the fertile mud, it runs down
his thighs, his calves, in his veins, and drops abruptly
from the knee below, while his ever-wakeful gaze
is all that manages to hold his body
steady as it sways, powerless to get free
even for the blink of an eye
from the venomous thorns—alive—a crown
of bees swarming everywhere around
his by-blow flower's brow—can they be gathering
pollen?—each one stings him
in hope that he might ascend in flight
for just an instant, dies,
then another comes to sting him, the hours
prick him like thorns, the swarming crown
renews itself in the air,

his pluricellular body is like honeycomb:
no longer does the cross hold him, nor his bonds,
nor the nails piercing his palms, only the crown
of bees as they swarm, to whom
the heavy honey and transparent wax,
the flesh of his drained body,
simply is

translated by
Adam J. Sorkin and Lidia Vianu

blood tie

outside little girls skip rope with a cord of blood

(he himself

put in their hands the circulation of his blood as a jump rope

—"since anyway you can't jump over yourself!"—they skipped rope

in turn with both feet together then with the left with the right, and they tripped

fell scraped themselves got to their feet whimpered and came in for

a good hiding—"since what mother dispenses helps you grow"—they wore out

their shoes wore out the cord against the asphalt it rained they kept on

jumping through puddles—"since blood is thicker than water"—they grew up

skipping the circulation of his blood   he himself

put in their hands the circulation of his blood as a jump rope

—"this life hangs by a thread"—they strung it

from two poles and hung to dry

their panties socks dresses   the wind

keeps twirling them round the rope as if the clothes

held on by their sleeves with clothespins were skipping

rope   in the yard—their little girls

caught up in the game—dresses ribbons—leaping about

like a clothesline in the gusts

of wind   an unsuspected blood tie

hidden within attaches itself

like the escutcheon of a newborn's

delicate hand like the label on the sleeve

of a coat   now while their mothers haven't yet called them in

haven't yet gathered them from the rope)

outside little girls skip rope with a cord of blood

translated by
Adam J. Sorkin and Lidia Vianu

Pietà (Ivy on the Cross)

ivy on the cross: vegetal blood
through arms spread wide
powerless, paralyzed
look at their veins, bulging,
bluish green: wooden crosses
the ancient aristocracy of cemeteries

ivy on the cross: passionate, sainted
Magdalene winding around the foot
of the stiff crucifix: from the cross
Jesus, nailed fast, stares transfixed by
her lithe body in which God
discovers Himself—*Aletheia!*—in the process
of photosynthesis: more air

for the cemetery (only six feet lies
underground—the rest rises in the open air
from the grass on the graves as high as
heaven: nothing but cemetery)

in spring: pious widows
keep coming to whitewash the arms
of the cross, which is bleeding (every March
the cemetery caretaker,
deeply religious, prunes
the green fingers like young branches
of both arms of the cross,
as he believes sacred and proper:

that each cross remain
a cross crucified in and of itself)

ivy on the cross: it doesn't want to know
about the caretaker, it doesn't want to know anything
Magdalene-ivy taking
each cross of fresh wood
for the Savior in the flesh
crucified upon Himself, ivy-
Magdalene winding around His arms
year after year—until one day they fall
to the earth's lap: *difficult is*

the descent of the cross from the cross.

translated by
Adam J. Sorkin and Stefania Hirtopanu

Electra

just to keep you current: I'm the one who plugs
two fingers in the socket and through the
electrical circuit stretches my hand deep into the night
feeling my way to you, your état d'âme and social
status—to be kept current—I enter houses
lit by one dim light bulb hanging down
from a ceiling bloated like a fetus recently aborted   I enter
rooms so brilliant with light that my
fuses burn out, spaces
where the light's never off and you can't
pull the sheet over your face, the bright-
ness is squeezed into your eyes like a lemon   I enter
the flashing dance-club light organ I'm ubiquitous in bathrooms
where seduced girls bend low over the sink
to overcome the nausea of carrying a child—and if you want to be kept current:

I'm the one who plugs two fingers in the socket
connected to the electrical grid I learn what
I come to know: this man opens the fridge more often
than he turns on the TV, that man listens (I can even feel his ear
glued to the radio) "to voices . . . ," under a neon sign a young couple
kiss, in an electric chair sa-
vonarola tears himself away electrocuted,
in the glow of a nightlight aged parents make love
while next door their offspring learn English from a porno flick,
loudspeakers blare, "I love you!" and at the very moment
when, caught in the wires, I find her at last, she
who turns the lamp off and smacks me across my fingernails

with a rod of darkness
then falls asleep

for those who want to be kept current: I'm the one who plugs
two fingers in the socket and through the *cir*(. . .)
and the (. . .)*coit* I reach her uterus—
her Magna Mater Energy   it feels
as if I'm making love by electrocution (*"it's so
hard to be married to electric light!"*),
conceiving fairy-tale princes of light
birth will be an electrical discharge, death
a short circuit of . . .   *"light! more light! . . ."*

to keep you current: I'm the one who
like a male kangaroo must penetrate
                            the socket with twin penises!

                    at night: alone
facing a white wall I hang
like a blanket over the window   the radio announces a blackout
and the curfew feels like a state of siege
with a black ribbon (of slogans) blindfolding my eyes: «свет в окне—
помощь врагу!»* the thousand and (l)one(ly) nights when you
aren't mine but—let me be kept current—at least
leave your light on for me, Electra

*translated by
Adam J. Sorkin and Lidia Vianu*

---

*(Russian) "Light in the window—aid to the enemy!"

pure blood

the pig asleep with its masters on the straw mattress as big as
a country stuffed alive   the peasants living amidst the stench
of the Christmas pig (the man crams straw into the corn-sacks his wife
sews their mouths shut so that they cannot tell how last
summer her man took the iron pitchfork and "stuffed"
the haystack while a boy and a girl— his very own daughter—were
making love in his hay!)—everybody's
ready for celebration: at the first glimmer
of dawn the peasant stabs the pig—there rises *un soleil cou coupé*
the pig struggles and soaks the mattress in blood (it winds up
looking like the empire at the time of ci-
V.I.L. war) damn! the straw—it's so soggy with blood—will not burn!
but glory be to god the oil lamp's close at hand: the peasant singes
the pig (as fresh blood sizzles in the straw! . . .)   so as not to waste
so much goodness in the straw he carries it to the cattle
pen (. . .) "wake up, ignat! . . . " his wife rouses him
terrified—from the manger can be heard a newborn's
thin whimper trickling down like a streak
of pure blood: "take the fork and go see!"

translated by
Adam J. Sorkin and Lidia Vianu

[almost transparent and I could see . . .]

almost transparent and I could see—like the metallic thread of a hundred-mark banknote,
                              discontinuously—
her spine. and the fact, so natural when it refers to somebody else, that she must die
was making her even more desirable. and I said nothing about the intrinsic value
of flesh—viewed in its *own* true *light*, its blaze, I could see
the watermark of the gods—those *beyond*
the pleasure principle (to write
about her and put to bed what's been set in type means in fact to put her
into circulation—out "in the light of day"—across the entire territory
of the distribution of language). and the fact
that she could be transformed was making her priceless (. . .)

                                        still, the time for the imperfect tense
has passed us by—like monetary reform in the ussr—overnight. she is.
and the present, but more than anything else the fact, naturally so commonplace, *that she*
                    must die
and she must suffer—that I cannot protect her—gives her this aura—
lacking a fitting word, I myself can only write—of poetry

                                        translated by
                              Adam J. Sorkin and Raresa Galaicu

[she dances on a sphere . . .]

she dances on a sphere   he sits on a cube

when she does splits it's as if the horizon line
were a rope that she skips

when she brings her hands together it looks as if
she were holding up her newborn baby for the first time: "it's a girl!" as if she
were playing with her as children play cat's cradle with string, careful
not to tangle the figure—so that
another child can take it, the same way

those other fingers can take the lifeline from his palm

translated by
Adam J. Sorkin and Lidia Vianu

[I'm speechless: she's the hopscotch grid . . .]

I'm speechless: she's the hopscotch grid that Jesus,

whenever a woman (always her again) taken in fornication is brought to him, *writes*

on the ground with his finger, and like a child she hops the ten commandments on one foot

from square to square from century to century through the second millennium

until she reaches number one, now exiting

the game. then it's his turn who is without sin to first cast a stone

into the hopscotch. so that the game

turns into a prayer of the heart: o Lord,

give us this day her body as you gave the people of Israel the decalogue

translated by
Adam J. Sorkin and Lidia Vianu

[when the universe was as big as the Hellas . . .]

when the universe was as big as the Hellas between your legs and I—the Greek in Thales'
       prayers whose phalanxes extended his sway over his colonies . . .
(the first and last lines are razorblades used by an elegant
woman to shave her armpits in turn till they thin to the pellucid azure of
eyelids shut tight over eyes of absolute-blue sea-dreams. in turn the woman
is a double-edge blade a man—the ad's "manly man"—prefers for shaving the split-ends of
       his nerves
that stipple his cheeks and jaws. when still very young, god shaved
for the first time, he used the double-edge blade—man and woman—that Plato described:
       "two faces
looking opposite ways," but he cut himself and blood flowed—holy blood? the devil's?—the
       razor
dropped from his hands. it's no secret who picked it up, who uses it now, who sometimes
       even
hones it ——————————————————————————————— I'm the
       sharpener:
I turn the gritstone wheel—*yellow sparks* leap forth—I'm like the Lumière brothers
       projecting
against a pristine bed sheet a man and a woman "in the passion of coupling oblivious to
       food
and everything else" and between them—call it what you will—the *pure form*. just like
a razorblade turned inside out with its edges furled inward: as if it blinked. and suddenly
the pure form fills with a sort of milky gaze, indistinct at first, then curious,
scrutinizing, bloodshot as if narrowly escaped from the dogcatcher, sleepy
and ultimately absent. the show's over. the sharpener rides off mounted on his gritstone.
taken out into the yard the next day the sheet flutters in the wind like the Japanese flag)

while the universe is no bigger than the Hellas between your legs and I—
the Greek in Thales' prayers whose phalanxes let slip away all his colonies one by one . . .

translated by
Adam J. Sorkin and Lidia Vianu

[from brain to sex the spine . . .]

from brain to sex the spine is designed to change gears like a bicycle chain, my love.

a bicycle named desire. the balanced

movement of her hand while she leads the way—as we ape

the beast with two backs—(shake off

your DNA chains)—I lightly stroke her vertebrae, then she slips

through my fingers like a bead necklace, a space-time continuum. pedaling in the nakedness

of her legs that chain me in *viparita maithuna*—while

along highway 69 ("the road of longing") we loop on

la tour de france—now accelerating, now clasping

her soles in pious prayer, and she communicates names to time: *Yin Time.* a response

comes like a reply—from the point of view

of *a corpse* ("then, oh, beauty! shout out to the vermin . . . ")—

like Ion Neculce: "worms, my god" she is not as I am and is when I am not. does life expectancy

in men show itself to be no more than a pair of bare legs

below the hem of an amazon's skirt? a nun's? a nun of death

translated by
Adam J. Sorkin and Lidia Vianu

[and then the figure with the scythe . . .]

and then the figure with the scythe swings his blade, slicing through
the middle of a verse, and says: "let this be your horizon
and your style! this eyebrow neither raised in astonishment, nor lowered.
under it you will drive your women ahead down the path into the poem from now on. each
walking tall, and none permitted to stand on tiptoe
to see beyond, or her head will be cut off, but they can't be laid flat on the ground
like grass mown by a scythe. as an example for my sisters, I'll go forward, shaved under the
          scythe."
and the women, who once dreamed of entering a verse, turn on their heels: toward dining rooms
and bedrooms, withdrawing to their own sex like eyes under eyelids, like the tongue
behind the teeth, like Cristian Popescu giving birth to his M-F'ing mother. there remains only
the scythe stuck in the middle of the verse, like the eyebrow
of a god, invisible and just, depending on how the wind blows. in the wind
— a weathervane—his eyebrow neither raised in astonishment nor frowning,
but showing which way his face will turn. always changing. *but luckily
the wind has stopped* . . . I'm no more than a point of view and he—the perspective!

                    —hey, goggle-eyes,
what can you see over there, far off, on the horizon?—the bald
soprano, may her luck be for god to spank her! she's busy combing her curls'
convolutions with a rake. her brain looks like mozart's peruke

*translated by
Adam J. Sorkin and Lidia Vianu*

[once I was a library rat . . .]

once I was a library rat: tasting
the host of the eucharist of her womanly body instead I turned into a bat.
between my bones—a membrane on which (by whose command?) *the garden*
of delights was projected—night has grown: with it, unfurled no less wide than eight time
zones across,
I glide over my lover's flesh, enfolding her body of supreme joy
the northern lights, barely veiling her holy trinity. she is
formed of space and time in a proportion (godly) of one to
three: but despite that, I dream to embrace all of her at once, like the tomb in which
through the power of transfiguration of her beauty, the worms,
metamorphosed into silkworms, will weave
the air with *The Assumption of the Virgin*

translated by
Adam J. Sorkin and Claudia Serea

[as in a story from the eighteen fifties . . .]

as in a story from the eighteen fifties—"candle flames
in the candelabras cast long gleams on rounded silver
dish-covers; the clouded facets of the cut crystal glasses
threw pale glimmers to one another . . . "—I set down
these words on a blank white page as if before the ball I'd fastened earrings
in an invisible woman's ears: at the level of her hearing.
that white night's score writes itself through my hands while they also
conduct the orchestra unexpectedly appeared—as if drawn out of a coat sleeve—to en-
liven, quite literally, the atmosphere, to add a brilliance to the party, the first
I took her to, but only after, piercing her ears, I hung
at the level of her hearing—carefully adjusting them in the little mirror of
the compact in which she keeps / I keep her face powder—the earrings with precious
stones, one carat each, the surfaces of those
polyhedrons with their cold sharp edges reflecting—at this moment (oh stay!)
a light flashed on—the squares of dancing couples. music! I followed each
turn in the waltz—levitating above the floor—how it enters into the bright play
of mirages in the jewelry, the dancers'
flesh—the white swan that can't tear its gaze away from
its self-mirroring borne towards the shore on a teasing wave—how
it acquires *a cold nervous edge* with the brass and piano and strings—in unison or
in succession, before the ball begins, like the jewelry
reflected in the little mirrors of the silver compacts—how into the ears
of each and every pair of dancers it pours the balm that *death is*
"for others," and she
—tidying her hair, with a gesture rehearsed at home until polished, staring into her partner's
eyes, unaware that he's nothing more than imaginary, the play
of the light and shadow from her earrings—how she draws within herself
how she loses herself waltzing among other reflections—mere specks of dust dancing

in the first rays the early morning sunlight, in the ballroom like a breath, if

after even the last servant has gone to sleep, are still real—how (from this point on, I follow her

only in my thoughts) she retires *chez elle*, she undresses—the perfume eva (. . .) vola-

tizes, the nameless body of lot's woman comes

to the surface, salt—how she ties her straps

—so that he can't see her—she touches the holes, now a bit wider, in her ears

—her partner was up to her level, her hearing: "*one*-two-three *one*-two-three . . . "—

how she lies down on the white page of the conjugal

bed—old age moves over, makes room for her

beside it: lukewarm comfortable pleasant—her eyes still fixed on

the earrings with their symmetrical slabs on the night table and

"she forced herself to stay awake in order to prolong the illusion of this

luxurious life . . . " ah, her flesh picks up a taste of rat

poison. I snatch it from the typewriter

and despite myself stuff it into my mouth: *madame bovary c'est*

moi

translated by
Adam J. Sorkin and Diana Manole

[I opened my eyes wide, and then . . .]

I opened my eyes wide, and then I felt it, my sight, plunging with my whole being head into
their double window.
her small fists banged against the stained glass of the medieval cathedral of my irises.
her breath like a teenager's waiting by the window clouded over my vision. with her
forefinger
she wrote S.O.S. in the center of that patch of mist that melted and
took it away, my scream. any art critic would have known instantly: munch's madwoman
contemplating (in one eye) on the white wall the shadow cast (in the other). once
I winked at her (in the mirror) with complicity—she turned her superb back on me, her spinal
column plaited in three, like a long braid tossed out the window so that her lover
can climb up to the garret. since then there hasn't been a day I've not felt her (watching out for
me) clasping to her breast
an icon of the Savior as—three steps forward three steps back—he gets closer to
and farther from the edge, seeing himself crashing down to
the pavement, as the drunken street sweeper describes it to the passersby
with a flourish the   t
r
a
j
e
c
t
o
r
y

o
f

the
f
a
l
l

translated by
Adam J. Sorkin and Lidia Vianu

[in my arms her body trembled . . .]

in my arms her body trembled all over—"they had told me I could not have a child!"—like an
eye between eyelids
on the verge of tears. invisible, pregnancy made her nauseous—a contact
lens—it made her look at the world anew, see what she'd never
before seen (including "the meaning of life"). her pupils, dilated
bigger than the red square during parades, tried in vain to hide from me—inside lenin's
mausoleum?—that
creaturely fear of death (not for herself, but for the species). I could see only the mausoleum,
only
little ilyich in his glass placenta. I remember in the hospital lobby
I kissed away her tears—as the poet says—with my lips and, as in the countryside, with my
tongue,
trying like a peasant to take the mote out of her eye. our daughter was born in april, like a
glance cast
out the window on a sun-filled day

translated by
Adam J. Sorkin and Lidia Vianu

["I think with my skeleton" . . .]

"I think with my skeleton," she'd say, and proceed to wash her hands thoroughly after every
touch
she was smooth as a river pebble. "I just don't understand
virgil mazilescu's fascination with *your distinctly feminine way of rotting*,"
and she'd proceed to wash her hands, "for I feel the weight of the earth, each speck
of dust fertilizing me like a fine yellow grain of pollen on a pistil.
I'm just as you see me, I'm hear-not, see-not, know-not. I'll never attain
perfection, the fourth dimension, of the maxim   S A T O R
                                                  A R E P O
                                                  T E N E T
                                                  O P E R A
                                                  R O T A S
                                                                except when
lowered into *the big square that has no corners*"

                    (. . .) one time I went
to a funeral. there were lots of people. we lined up to throw
a handful of earth into the grave as is our custom, returned home from the dead man
had dinner watched the news got into bed between the sheets—and she hadn't even
                                    washed her hands!—we made love
like never before as if she had no bones, turned off the light. in the dark
we clasped hands, two deaf-mutes, puzzling in our minds: that handful of earth,
which of the two of us will be left to throw it into *the big square that has no corners*, for the
                    other? . . .

translated by
Adam J. Sorkin and Lidia Vianu

[about the "history of the illness" . . .]

about the "history of the illness" or the x-ray I can say nothing more.
it may be a japanese
engraving of living tissue: a small branch of blood trembling in the gentlest
breeze, the petals of leucocytes
                    falling
                        " . . . *in aeternam*"

translated by
Adam J. Sorkin and Lidia Vianu

[the thermometer in my armpit: as if a transfusion . . .]

the thermometer in my armpit: as if a transfusion of quicksilver for

(presumed) inward mirrors. 102.6° F. fever. my body turns to one side, then the other

like a kaleidoscope that changes from red glass (embers) to

emerald (cold shivers) with a twist, then back. while

the fever grows, my legs poke beyond the covers, stiff like two parallel

tram lines that lead (or led, more precisely) to

the central cemetery, where with bare feet they search in the dark

for a clay boot somebody else happens to be wearing at the moment but are

unable to find it and hurry back underneath. fever. the house warm

again after a trip to africa—no, that's not kindling,

just the creaking of my joints—from which I narrowly escaped,

my skin hung on a stick like the last (white) flag of the race. it's getting dark. *I, myself.*

my entire being contracted within my sleepy eyelids against my pupil watching the sky's
            kaleidoscope

through the airplane window. one movement and the northern hemisphere

flips upside-down. "careful! don't touch it!"

it's my daughter who's carrying to my bed a cardboard tube

with mirrors, god's eight-point star. "show it to mother." the mirror

on the retro wardrobe—can this be dream?—brings her before me. silent film.

merry-go-round with. faces gestures bits of glass. mother daughter. at the other end of.

"what do you see?"   "add these."   the jewelry box (most of them fake—this last,

for thieves to take note of) contributes its contents to the kaleidoscope. silver symmetries

golden honeycombs sparkles like water glitter

of diamonds. after a day like this it's comforting to see *la*

vie en rose (your own), relaxing at the end of—a dream journey? a nightmare?—to close
            your eyes in your own bed,

assuring yourself: "I'm falling asleep." And I am falling asleep, the thermometer in my
            armpit. the last thing I hear before

I enter the tunnel is her voice chanting vowels—*A noir E blanc I* . . . —at the (presumed) end of. "how come you're not writing about the kaleidoscope?"

translated by
Adam J. Sorkin and Lidia Vianu

[I'll go (they'll carry me) . . .]

I'll go (they'll carry me) on my final journey. The lost path. Through the forest
of symbols. Suddenly the guide will call out: "pit-stop!—skeleton to
the right, flesh to the left. One minute only! Whoever's late must catch up with the cortège on
foot."
I can almost see them: each in the other's arms, they can't bear to be separated. In vain the
guide
hurries them: "*strong and stiff*—on your right, *slender and soft*—in the direction
of your left hand," each in the other's arms they can't get enough of their caresses. "*yin*—to
the left,
yang—to the right" but they can't be pulled apart from their hugs. The cortège
scolds them: "now is when you find time to embrace?" they're disgusted at them: "even where
everyone can watch . . ." bring back the dead from the grave, while those two
hurry ahead *towards the forest* like a bride to bed. the skeleton whispers nothings
in the flesh's ear (I can almost hear it):
"damn it, *ma chère chair*, what can I say / last night you were eager, but not today?!"

translated by
Adam J. Sorkin and Lidia Vianu

[gesture in white: the unmade gesture . . .]

gesture in white: the unmade gesture—half unborn half dead—knocks over
the ink bottle. the spilled ink spreads over the page can't
stay in place draws its knees to its mouth gathers itself and at last
stands up like an ebony statuette
bought in madagascar and out of which the model
naomi strides forth. ah! her feet scissor time I didn't even notice when
she withdrew backstage leaving the whiteness as if untouched. the cadaverous
pallor of this unwritten sheet of paper lifts its bed in its arms and
—"lazarus, come forth!"—rises from the
dead, leaving an empty space.
what remains there loses heart and by chance opens the umbrella
of a question mark. the regret
after *it wasn't meant to be* lasts to the next period.

poetry is like death on the bridal bed and birth on the deathbed

translated by
Adam J. Sorkin and Lidia Vianu

[good god! I'm no longer . . .]

good god! I'm no longer an obstacle even to my own blood. it burst out
through my nose and mouth, leaving me behind like a wall, rather rougher and
wetter than white like chalk. "rise up," I commanded it, "and
walk!" it looked like it was out of a book, an anatomical
diagram: vein aorta artery . . . 5 liters of blood from
the circulatory system stood at attention (I'd write "stark
naked" if they hadn't renounced the body altogether), while the vein and the radial
artery were trying—instinctively—to cover the sex as if before a military
enlistment board. it suddenly made an about-face and I could tell
that it was departing since its shadow of air woven by nuns in văratic monastery grew smaller
on the wailing wall that remained. there followed
a dozen guys (he gave them to drink, he said: "drink, all of you, for this
is my blood . . . "), just as the cinnabar majuscule is followed by
uncials in identical long dark soutanes, from deciphering
which you, *mon semblable mon frère*, will learn that
not a drop of his blood
remained uninscribed

translated by
Adam J. Sorkin and Lidia Vianu

[resting with her head in the sun with her feet in the moon . . .]

resting with her head in the sun with her feet in the moon, she gives birth to a day of light. and
I, how can I be extinguished?
I clasp light to my chest as if, in darkness, I were embracing an adolescent
body half still half clad in black clothes, just like the clay church in căuşeni *The Assumption
of the Virgin*, enough to take the place of a mother. a head resting above (severed from) the bare
shoulders
of the horizon, *premier danseur* attendant upon his partner when—*one*-two-three—the day
glides *en pointe*
to the zenith when—carried by many hands—she exits offstage, and her soles (parentheses
that frame like a reckoning, separated by the hyphen of sex, birth and death dates) are new
moon
old moon, the man's head is—with dawn's forceps, a high-precision instrument, nickel and
blood / with sunset, the axe's
edge (when we say axe we are thinking of raskolnikov)—cracked apart
like a marble bath / porcelain trough / clay tub in which the ideal
woman (cf. *the male brain*) splashes in his specter—what would you like to drink: the wave or
the sea?—and the waves
bear her naked form to the shore. to write as you breathe. as you'd give
mouth-to-mouth resuscitation to the water creature tossed upon the shore, who (no longer)
dreams of the sky, until
she kisses you back / you feel her tongue in your mouth, first a stranger's, then like your own.
until diaphragm
transforms to placenta. may the word you utter be *the one born,
not made*

*translated by
Adam J. Sorkin and Lidia Vianu*

[the blinds—my face is a grater . . .]

the blinds—my face is a grater on which god shaves light from his face—filter the vespers
into the notebook, sketching lines of moving shadows, that I can feel
with my fingertips like a blind man. I write on the line of the extinguished. aslant. with the haste
of a man who—like pavlov on his deathbed dictating to his medical students
about his end, still living—didn't have any idea how long
he'd been working on his posthumous works. hands, or maybe not hands—the invisible
caresses of armorers or lens polishers in amsterdam
put circles under my eyes my face in shadow stuff my insides
with darkness, where I retreat and die. writing for
four hands follows (*allegro, ma non troppo*) with—the blinds cast a "zebra"
of light and shadow across the page, precious keyboards or bar lines—
fugit irreparabile tempus, the same as in literature
the man-in-the-iron-mask, his cranium like a poppy pod still green scored
all around so that, milky and bland to the taste, can be extracted the sleep filled with
dreams of greatness, he stared out between the bars into the void. just as between the blades
of the confessional of lines, poetry is a look high into the heavens by someone
who is confessing—to anyone/no one—or, cast down to the ground, the heavy
look of one forgiving—anyone/no one—in contumacy. when invisible hands quickly draw
the blinds down, when (the same?) hands (without end), in silence, make a new
clean copy of it, as if you were clothing the dead body in predestined clothes
(the striped pajamas of light hung and forgotten on the coat rack):

my face is merely a grater on which god shaves light from his face, till nothing's left

translated by
Adam J. Sorkin and Lidia Vianu

[and I've embraced a poetics . . .]

and I've embraced a poetics—just like the leper embraced one day by francis of assisi:
from my texts there fell almond-shaped pieces of living, rotting flesh—epithets. where beauty
struck me a bruise appeared ripened came to a head till it burst.
through a gap as between the slats of a fence, without meaning to I saw
hounds sniffing all around me snarling snapping their teeth at the pieces
of flesh freshly fallen in sadness. I've read every book. I married off
my poem to the first comer. not a month later I went to ask
how it feels to be married among strangers. then, you know, she:
"for shame and for fear / I'm fine daddy dear." yet, did I not
have the gall? did I not presume? to ask again: "oh daddy's girl
you're not so frail / what makes you as thin as a rail?" because I'm always
in a frantic rush. morning and evening I go to the public baths. thrice
I've renounced my impure body in that very marriage bed of her
supreme joy. now where once my epithets had fallen
the black loam has grown rich dogs eat their fill orchids
bloom on either side of my poetics, the narrow footpath along which I lead
my body hand in hand with death—lest it go astray or feel afraid—
like a younger brother led the first time to his first woman. then a herd
of swine crosses my path and implores, "send us into your brother, let us
enter him." "*go!*"

translated by
Adam J. Sorkin and Rareșa Galaicu

passager

so what if from time to time he opens his veins? he belongs to the chosen species, those who
sharpen their blood that way.

red-blue. at both ends. like a bicolor pencil. turning blue in the pencil sharpener

of the heart, until it forms a point. from the way it nips at the fingertips, from inside-out, with
little red horns,

ready to assert *non omnis moriar*, ready to write. half in the hands of the Lord, half given over
to the devil—but no one's ever contented

with a half-measure! and cut by the knife's blade, the dividing line no longer seems certain.

as if, tossed up like an inlaid cane, it would be contested in the space of a game's opening play,

by two different hands, thrusting higher at the same moment they meet somewhere in the
middle. each

against the other, writing brings them closer: on hot coals, the demon (said to be "of
creation") turns into a prodigality of purple

as high above as God, just as, the graphite that he has instead of a heart running out, that
God is what nearly

goes to the devil! not much is needed until one will start to write with the other's blood,
gothic broadswords in confrontation under banners

in the glagolitic. for life and death. as in a complete litany of names—the exact same—passing
in turn from *the ones*

[*the dead*] to *the others* [*the plowmen*]: not a letter isn't written twice, with cinnabar and with
bluing, once in the heavens and, then turned back,

on earth. from the taste of rust in my mouth, ever more pronounced, it seems that they've
already begun to slash each other with swords dripping
with blood.

now growing weaker, with double-edged blades, they grab hold first of one, then of the other,
with bare hands.

within this hand-size homunculus, God and Satan arm-wrestle. the homunculus

writes in ink for the dead
and for the living in red

translated by
Adam J. Sorkin and Claudia Serea

passagère

following her, I remembered only her going by. Her walk, as if she wore an almost ripe
                pomegranate (in Romanian, *rodie*, in French, *grenade*) between her
                thighs: struck
by her beauty, no further back than for three generations, you could hear her blood pulsing
                at her wrists like a bracelet
of hot rubies—all that's remained after a revolution, two wars and recently, in these
                widowed times, from her
family's inheritance—on the inside, right to the bone—her delicate bones: through them,
                death sips
its cocktail (sap) of marrow—with a little straw of DNA. a garden enclosed in seeds of
                punica grana-
tum—through the reddish-pink pulp of the grains, the white seeds revealed like girls
                displaying themselves
in the windows of the red-light district in Amsterdam—one of them answering to the
                name—pure little pomegranate—rodica

(a word so commodious that if you press your ear to it, you can hear a heart beating, and
                round, deep inside, two pregnancies).

a closed circle. a man following a woman as on a watch the minute hand chases after the
                second hand.
a woman passing. a passerby—under her feet the hours lie like a pedestrian crosswalk's
                zebra stripes—drenched in honey through which you saw the *lou-*
minosity of day/at the end of which—it doesn't have one!—she undresses for you, *in toto,*

vanitas vanitatum et omnia vanitas. without passing by—in her steps, the pavement rattles
                its armor like a dragon's
tail's "here I am!" the scales—with the neck's shadow—all the matter she has in it—which
                draws her
to the other side—*sic transit . . .*—on music by—don't tell me!—*noir désir*, the ecclesiast's
                voice—"*le vent nous
portera*" de-
          scend-
              ing, as you'd divide a word into syllables, to pass it from one line to
the next, the steep escalator stairs that the flesh climbs at a run, out of breath
(clean black earth, her flesh—*"don't stare at me that I'm black . . . "*—through which, gracefully,
                her veins manifest themselves as,
swelling after a rain, rosy earthworms from out of the ground.) and the ultimate expression of
                the brevity of her going by:
taking the metro at piața romană and getting off after a couple of stops at place pigalle.

passagère. where she sits still, her sex cuts—through living flesh—on the life line—the original
meridian. greenwich. and on both sides of it, her thighs—two time zones—
held tightly closed, make a perfect Y (as in Yin), a martini glass—tossed with an insouciant
                gesture the olive
that will never fall, her navel—I drink the nights—"don't take it away from me . . . "—and
                the days I drink I drink and I drink.
only she doesn't stay still. she's one
with the line of the horizon—just as her panties with the names of the days
of the week: *monday, tuesday, wednesday . . .* on the vertical. one beside another twelve lines
                forming,
unwillingly, the bar code of the kingdom of heaven. when she walks away, the lines carry
                between her legs—the tran-
scendental caesura that gapes wide, letting be seen . . . —the sonnet
of innocence lost along with its final line:

enclosed garden, sister, bride, forbidden well . . .
nobody stands witness when the gardener, prun-
ing, places in a girl's body the *puni-*
ca granatum seed with her first blood—each girl
in her flowering is his dream—it will sprout,
he'll watch it grow, bear fruit—then in dance, set loose,
he*rodia*s like a chain explosion whose
wave is the blush on her cheeks—to burst out,
past bounds!—then fill the expanse of time/space *hic*
et nunc. out in the world, on untasted lips, is
carmine (upper)/*de sable* (lower), the abyss.
you can see through her evening dress—*dessous chic*—
her shahid belt. and torn off, her finger, its ring

....

translated by
Adam J. Sorkin and Claudia Serea

sang d'encre

all your ancestors since way back when, each darker than the other, grew nothing more than
darkness, under the name of blackest earth, waiting to see (like a candle in the east)
illumination rise. just as you strike a match to check that you haven't forgotten a lit candle
            overnight,
so the apparition reveals itself: its head empty, like a halloween pumpkin, and inside, from
            the top of its head,
hanging like a hundred-watt bulb, the wonder-child, now extinguished, now more dazzling
than ever, going head to head with you: little no-bort boy, alive according to the year of his
            birth.
"what's your name, miracle of a city-hall decree?"
                                        —if he'd own up to a name,
on account of how many times it would be repeated, myself I'd hate being on everyone's
lips, and yet (pointing a finger at him, "come here! . . . "). "tell me, who's
your father . . ."
            "whose boy are you, little sin?"
                        "no one's!"

none of your ancestors, each brighter in the east than the other, can
see him through the monocle of the eclipse of the sun, only through
the pince-nez of an eclipse of the sun and moon, and even then from quite a ways off, as if their
            stares
got lost at the horizon like high tension wires. they could only think: how could they burn out
his filament, how, not at all in a rhetorical sense, could they wring his neck—and exchange him
            for ilyich's
lamp! unless he makes use of what might be under the lampshade of your skull,
deploys you as a searchlight to blind their vision.
so they all cast down their eyes.
then blackest earth fills their eyes.

and the dust of the field, so light and gentle, opens arms wide and welcomes them.
the dust spreads its legs: *". . . never mind my being so black!"*

"we must show respect for the ways of the ancestors!" they exclaim, both one and the other, the
        dark and the
bright east-born, your people before you. since you are wise, with a single voice they invite you
        take a seat
at the head of the table. and then to stand on the table—the wonder-child
sees the world upside-down; don't look him in the eye, he'll make you fall down!—if
you can't reach him, get up on a chair too, that's why you've been invited, only after you've all
        put a hand on him
can those down below start turning the table round, clockwise: "when the clock strikes one,
the black man comes . . .", at the end of the count, you're amazed to see, instead of treading
        the earth
with feet on the ground, they themselves soar into the sky, legs fluttering in the air like tassels.
together, the dark beside the bright east-born, hands fixed upon
the glossy table top, as at a requiem, cradled by *rest in peace*!
like a last supper borne into the firmament, with apostles and the whole shebang—and raised
        high above. ascended into glory—
what can be seen from underneath isn't hands clasped in prayer on the tablecloth, but
how they keep kicking under the table—on a scale of one to ten,
                one to one hundred,
                  one to one thousand . . .

now, since it's good riddance to them all one after the next, you cannot avoid what you most
        feared:
you sit there at the table on your chair, your head in its hundred-watt halo, stained by flies,
waiting for the preparations to be completed—the bulb blinks in complicity, the wonder-
        child glows
with pleasure, until a bright dot appears on your forehead, as if
a sniper had you in his sights—at long last the film's ready to begin. The lights dim.

On a white sheet stretched taut between maternity and morgue, the words THE END replace
                the one that reads it, now even with closed eyes. In the dark. The credits
follow it (relatives, friends, a band of comrades). Spooling backwards,
your life in diminution. Other sheets, between which you uttered other names. Some have
                even come to life.
Exchanging one whiteness for another. Names you've forgotten. Your first time.
Interminable sleepless nights when you dreamed of a woman but had only
(the black and white film breaks from time to time. Catcalls! Whistles! . . .)
two sharing one bed, you and your brother. one mother for both, never just yours.
arm in arm, hand in hand, a little hand, held in arms . . . you hadn't realized that, look,
you're watching animated cartoons. somebody's flipping through the pages of the family
album: "oh! the wonderful child . . . " which leads—when all's said and done—to wonder-child.

was that child you? did the nickname *wonder* . . . to you?

you're in the middle of the house, bare-bottomed. they don't give a damn. you're—just one extra
to your parents—like a milk tooth tied to a door handle, watching the front door,
when someone yanks it open and—*blitzlicht*—there on the threshold.
a woman, in *contre-jour*—the sun suffuses her golden silhouette—through which
you yourself foresee in her bitter weeping that
not a single doctor, no one would . . . "however shall I make do, mama, with two of them?!"
you've never been more frightened. from that terrible shock
comes self-consciousness, striking you on the crown on the head: "I am the other!"

day. year. signed: *the law's little no-bort boy*

translated by
Adam J. Sorkin and Lidia Vianu

langue au chat(te)

"Les autres ils disent comme ça
Qu'elle est trop belle pour moi
Que je suis tout juste bon
A égorger les chats
J'ai jamais tué de chats
Ou alors y a longtemps
Ou bien j'ai oublié
Ou ils sentaient pas bon
Enfin . . . "

Jacques Brel, "Ces gens-là"

cerebral to the degree that it (poetry) doesn't make a sound while it crosses the mind, I offer
my temple
as a buffer. this means that death wipes her mouth with our first names.
(when once in a while we happen to bump into each other—hi! what's up?—
through the silk of her stockings I can hear the clinking of her bones, whiskey on the rocks.)
considered coldly, such that the cerebral
hemispheres huddle together like a cat and dog that all their lives have eaten
from the same bowl—the dog howls as if over a dead soul. the cat
has seven lives—but now they've reached its bottom and overturned it on their heads. about
fear of death
I can only hiss out of one side of the mouth as my teeth chatter
against the lip of the glass that's my own body, with 30 percent thirst
for life and the rest 70 percent water in which there's a set of false teeth floating, left
overnight. just like the cheshire
cat, playing at transparence—ending with the grin. from ear to ear (this is
between us, girl to girl—what-hasn't-a-body-penetrates-what-hasn't-a-
slit expressed in another dialect: in one ear and out the other). in the form of
a boomerang (closed parentheses). smacking me across the face: "smile! say cheese!"
it happens that the grin-sans-pussy sends me kisses from my childhood. "go 'way! scat!" (a
shameful disease,

this childhood: it always has to be hidden until our dotage, when one's mind seems to
return

to second childhood.) "dogs, not kids!"—the words conjugate like dogs mating until they
reach our ear.

a fond pairing of words. something between son of a bitch and a mole rat.

they mean "screw your birth and your mother's too!" muttered through his teeth, and they
mean

sweets at the tail end. funeral sweets.

it's supposed to be a sunny afternoon, with the poem that breaks the cat in your teeth.
actually,

it's a night with a full moon that makes "dogs,

not kids!" shove the cat-in-the-bag. inside—a bag of bones, outside—living skin.

little orphan veronica turned upside-down on her back flinging *the massacre*

of the innocents in your face: two fatherless little girls, 6 and 9 years old, maria and ioana,

stab their shovels into the bag tied at the mouth lest it breathe a word, and it wriggles in the
dust

like a crumpled draft of t. s. eliot's *the waste land*, on which you can barely read

half a line: "And I will show you . . . "—pure heroin, the children's cruelty. as much cruelty

as poetry—hide-and-, to the best of their limited capacity. like the scab on a wound, sight:
the blood

clots into vision. so majestic that in order to get with it from the first moment and not miss

anything—knots like a fist in your eye, like a clod with eyes, like a child's head—you
absolutely must

open your eyes with forceps. the cat becomes the cloth. like the background layer, as if
you've peeled a raw egg, your pallor

covering the screen. a cataract over the eye. and the film that's never stopped running

(just like dostoevsky, a cloth sack on his head, it was in '49, the 22nd of december, living
through «десять ужасных, без-

мерно страшных минут ожидания смерти»*, at the end of which—so they say—he was

never the same) for thirty years and more. and the fact that

---

* (Russian) "ten endless, horrifying minutes waiting for death"

you've not told anyone, as if—pussyfoot it outa here!—it were no fault of your own,

pardon my Latin: *hic jacet* . . . slaked lime. (just like your skin showing through the raw-
                                             eggshell ground layer

as goose bumps!) it shows that death retracts her claws in the diphthong's paw.

it's called *je donne ma langue au chat*. sometimes

I give her *langue à la chatte*.

(like a black fingernail that grows and grows and grows and after that . . . the tongue in the
                                             mouth.)

delivered by hand to the scary man with the sack from childhood.

smack in the kisser: "there at the priest's front gate

                       his mangy dead cat waits

                       laugh out loud or speak or sing

                       into its mouth you spring."

translated by
Adam J. Sorkin and Lidia Vianu

une histoire d'amour: la dame aux ours

music: serge gainsbourg
voices: serge gainsbourg/jane birkin

any woman, no matter how old she seems, is younger if she has a little girl who sports a red
scarf once a month—"just call me bloody-little-angel"
(when the girl won't show up, she must be expecting). a man, no matter how young he wants
to appear, is older
with a marriageable girl (till she goes off to her own home, she's a burden in his). *"tes vingt
ans, mes quarante . . . "*
oh! when it happened the first time, it was like the red square—everywhere u.s.s.r. flags
from head to foot (between the legs, rather), so at the predestined hour
bloody-little-angel never made her appearance. an absence fraught with consequences, as the
girl had to make her bed
under the knife. it wasn't so much the scars—as the cutting of living flesh: *"you, who had wed
virginity
to nativity"*—it was the clatter of metal instruments
that took him months to forget. even now, whenever he goes to her,
he hears the bell-like clinking of tubes, the curette at work within a copper uterus. *"ça
c'est l'histoire . . . "*

        (yin)discreet to the nth degree. a laundry room where all the girls in a student
dorm have spread their
underwear to dry—their sex multiplied to the horizon as far as the eye can see, like a flight of
swallows heralding dawn—her flesh, after a night of lovemaking. always open to a goodly
tumble. if only it weren't for the fear one might upset the bloody-little-angel (and this
after he's already left her dangling once . . .) you're really happy
when she tells you on the phone: "my *urşi* are here, my little bears!" (her words
break the silence like the red-dyed eggs that get knocked against one another at easter:
"Christ has risen!" symbolized in red,

the calendar days of their love: "truly, he is risen!")

never called by her name, a call of the blood.

   (gathered into two braids, then drawn in a circle, parted in the middle—hers. she unplaits it
   once a month, as if she spliced all four sundays into one. on the way
   down the path—swelling under the skin, his. as if entering his skin. so as not to be twisted
   in the dna chains tugging in opposite directions   —*"Tourne-toi*
                                          —Non
                                          —Contre moi . . . "
   hers turns versus minus, his versus plus. rhesus-conflict.)

a woman wanders by, and at once a man claps his hand on his forehead, a gesture that
                                expresses: "you
read my mind!" a man comes along, and a woman takes him within the parentheses of her
                                thighs, to give birth to him
or to his child. oh! and it's over before it begins, when it happens.
out of the blue, outside the latex of the nightcap. at the other end of the red line, each time,
they count silently the days before.   "*—Oh mon amour . . .*
                            —L'amour physique . . . " (their mating
translates into zoological terms: *un ours mal léché*, he, and—unless in heraldic—*la dame aux*
                                    ours, her.

an age-old literary motif: *la belle et la bête*. you go to bed with a woman and wake up in a fairy
                                  tale with bears
where the girl lets herself be kidnapped by the beast and taken to the likewise virgin forest, to
                            the den which she changes
into a cave.) "my *urşi* are here . . . " (exactly the same as in olden days
when the bear appeared to her the first time in her childhood sleep. asleep, the beauty and the
                          dream—a wet dream.)

   love, a tale of blood.

(the iron she has in her blood, it's enough for a cage to keep her bears locked up
while he counts the bars, knocking on each of them with his rod.
so much iron circulates in his blood, he can erect scaffolding all around
the tower in which, behind a door with seven locks, she's waiting for him at the bars of
the window. in a hurry to strip off her striped
pajamas. *si j'ai quoi affirmatif et quoi d'autre . . . no comment*")

a woman («дай бог не последняя!»*). the first man. *"in a concelebration unto consummation."*
                              death
leaves them cold, for they're in heat. lying on her back, under him, eyes wide open, she dreams
that their love pushes ursa major across the heavens/pushes the little stroller across the heavens.
                              each is more alone than the other.
he pulls her on top. in seventh heaven he sees (how far?
so very near!)—*d'azur, à sept étoiles d'or*—ursa minor. and they both, one and the other, think of
the great bear, back home. at that point, the bloody-little-angel comes back from wherever she has
                              been—this
is her origin: open up!— cotton candy in her hand—"surprise!"—and she sticks out
her red tongue. so much for co-operative-pulation

                                        translated by
                                        Adam J. Sorkin and Lidia Vianu

---

* (Russian) "may God let it not be the last!"

(po)em in flesh and blood

—*first voice*
—*second voice*

when I'm about to turn the corner, it should happen the same way that in the scaffolding
that girdles the *trei ierarhi* monastery, wood and iron overlap and intertwine. "i'll never turn the
corner so long as
her roundness, in my disc-jockey hands, plays the music of the spheres."
"just the same way that rust and woodworms marry (with white bridal sails) till kingdom
come." "more than anything else,
the saying *even if i don't have, I still give!* best suits her, when in my arms she takes me between
parentheses." "the same way that boys and girls form a circle, holding each other around their
shoulders/their waists, dancing the *hora*,
with an embroidered girdle from the *trei ierarhi*." "chaining me/chaining her, around arms and
legs, with a dna chain."
"each girdle, its own pattern; no two alike!" "and there's no one without a pair." "all around,
an iron forest rises out of the church's stone, full of wrinkles, as if it meant to give god
a facelift." "closer and closer, love (never has she gone
to church, my darling) concelebrates with me unto consummation." "iron scaffolding
in a geometric pattern, wood scaffolding in a vegetal pattern, corresponding to
each girdle; knee-high scaffolding." "reaching perfection takes palpable forms
when, drenched with sweat passing through a shock wave, her skin gathers in timeless designs
not necessarily geometrical, but vegetal." "and then, after the scaffolding's dismantled, look, no
church at all."
"i'll sock you one you can't stand up to! *even if i don't have, I still give!*"

translated by
Adam J. Sorkin and Diana Manole

60

pure/purer

1. ♂

not so much about the takeoff, but rather about raising high—*hosannas!*—her runway itself for
        the flight to seventh heaven,
in a room rented by the hour, (three times) with an eye on the clock, on a wedding trip (to
        heaven) chi(și)nău—beijing, *via* vienna,
when (along with reaching cruising altitude) the temperature doesn't decrease but increases,
        and your boeing (judging by the gland) transforms itself,
as it advances, into a concorde preparing—*at a terrifying speed*—its final explosion

and not so much about defying gravity, but rather about not getting it—as the french would
        say: not falling—pregnant,
in a wedding bed raised, through the presence of the female sex, to the power of motherland,
when your spinal column/her vertebrae have already switched to high frequency, a duet, and
        the automatic
pilot can't find enough of a landing strip to put down under the feet not of heaven, but rather
        of heaven's gate between the thighs

2. *via*

"viens! viens!" vienna—that's how she was secretly called, and the way a vein would throb
        like a *blue danube* on her forehead
placed her not so much on the political atlas, but rather—even in the absence of the empire,
        a beloved capital!—on a geophysical
relief-map (praise be to natural formations!). landing only for as long as needed to make you
        fly again—no departures/arrivals except *via* vienna!—,
her arching over you also like nut over geb. her, a high-voltage arc, while you. and if

she comes, a rainbow. a quick one, at first, and later—5 time zones, 8 hours of flight—to
                                the end of the night
("even when we're in synch, you do it contrary to the light and I according to the sun"),
                                plus or minus
the time difference. all airline routes, —his/the lounge at the same airport, hers (its name
could be read on her lips— *"viens! viens!"*—, even if you stare straight into her eyes, even if
                                you lower your gaze). even beyond
desire, he/not beneath his pleasure, she. at his highest altitude, he/in depth, she. pure/
                                purer. plucked from paradise,
the runway's for taking off/blue like *via*[gra], the heavens

3. ♀

love is . . . when, excavated from the great square with no corners, a cube of
black earth (mine) tumbled in sync with
a black cube (yours) of earth and, finally stopping, show on the surface
my skull your skull—white dots of bone—coming up 1:1

or when, the grave turned mouth downward on the green felt of the grass two bone
dice (my skull your skull) tumble out in sync, in their movement
knocking together embracing until they give birth to a third. at rest, they come up
—black dots of soil, the earth in the mouth in the nostrils in the eye sockets—6 and 6 and 6

translated by
Adam J. Sorkin and Diana Manole

Bessarabian Fugue

the earth stuck to our feet with books (ours) of clay
(scraping against the trees) our shoes coming untied,
first one lace then the other, first nistru then prut, while we . . .   *allegro.* god's pedal
floors the accelerator and barely taps the brakes from time to time
pumps every gasp of our breath into a gas pipeline, the trans-si-
beria-n pipeline through which
day and night pumped by the (same?) pedal the last breath of
ten thousand people marched *pohod*
na sibir flows back home in order to flicker
in the stove-burner's eye, a triple/quadruple icon lamp warming *(our)*
daily (lead us not . . .)   my name should be
bejenaru. so help me
god. I survived tartars and turks, but how can I escape the devil
himself when, after my flight, I find him in the act of fleeing
that is in my very name. bejenaru. *bezanije.*   *presto:*

the flight itself cut in two   the fugue itself cut in two
as by the hunting   as by the hunting

rifle like   rifle like
two shots in one   two shots in one

the field itself cut in two   the field itself cut in two
upon which falls   upon which falls
the flight itself cut in two   the fugue itself cut in two

the body itself cut in two   the body itself cut in two

on both riverbanks   on both riverbanks
running upstream   running upstream
and downstream   and downstream
now nistru then prut untying   now nistru then prut untying
me   missa

                                                solemnis

I can't be a postmodernist, I won't be, I'm shy. (Ave) Maria had
nine princely sons. on a monday
she baptized them, on the next day she counted them and of the nine eight remained,
of the eight, seven, of the seven (so on and so forth) until of the last one, none—the fate
of all peoples who can neither read nor write. in a
small country stained everywhere with ink, what kind of ink would
you have for your small country? red! god
inscribes the dead in black ink, and the living in red.
the mothers left the east going west,
each carrying a bundle with brains.
group after group. *brain-drain.* guess who carried me
thirty-three
years (revolutions) ago? I was born in flight. since mother
gave birth to me in the lap of the homeland. the hammer
and sickle were the monograms on her red skirt. I've
escaped the hammer and sickle, but not the purple of
indecent skirts hiked up—"eat me!" how to escape?! . . .   with confiscated earth
stuck to my feet with books (ours) of clay and
straw on my shoes, our shoes coming untied,
first one lace then the other, first nistru then prut. I have made my
boots out of blackest soil. now I could exclaim (thirty-three
years after Sylvia Plath): motherland,
black shoe in which I have lived like a foot

having learned to walk to the cadence of a foreign language. I can't
even say which foot is which. but so as not to lose the cadence, I whisper to myself:
one at nistru!
one at prut!

translated by
Adam J. Sorkin and Lidia Vianu

civil war

to nicolae pojoga

"if a tongue signifies a people—as we know too well, the people sit ready for good and bad,
their bottom in two boats at once / *the boat with two
bottoms*—
both life and death join in one and the same word: the word *război*, the loom and the war."
the photographer came straight from the front lines: " . . . and so I wonder, for what am I a
correspondent?—weaving on the loom? a war
to defend territorial integrity?" the front line—
like a bi-color typewriter ribbon—
leapt to one side of the nistru, then the other. red and black,
wounded and dead on both sides. like the shuttle of a loom,
charon's boat ferried back and forth between the riverbanks. it was the year '92. the nistru
border
had broken, the zipper had got stuck between bender and tiraspol
where—if you look at the map of the republic—the fly should be,
and snagged in its iron teeth, the male member.
"the same word was also what the rug that hung on the wall was called, decorating the big
house
like an iconostasis in which the wedding photo of the holy family would appear;
as well as a more recent one, the son in the army." the old man knew what he was talking
about, not for nothing had he been married twice;
"this is the way the world's always been—men head off to war that looms, women weave on
the loom. in short, *the iliad* and
the odyssey!" the women between the two fronts went on strike along the railroad tracks
against the latin alphabet and the romanian language, blocking the trains going east,
as if, what woe! adopting the latin alphabet could change life's
track gauge. (even though nobody has reset its switches since then!)
after they'd bound all the men of the nation in traditional towels, as at a wedding, in '89 and

'91, during great national gatherings,
the women wondered if now they had enough linen or towels for themselves.
(so many bridges over the nistru—tenfold, even a hundredfold—bridges for the last journey!)
the photographer stuck to his idea—"wouldn't it be more correct to say the *război* that is civil
is only the weaving loom? . . . " when the volunteers & carabiniers failed to keep
their appointment *pro patria mori*, reservists were mobilized—
and so it was that I myself narrowly missed entering this poem feet first,
urged by—may he rest in peace—grigore vieru: " . . . there's still lots of room under the cossack
bullets. better go down (I really saw myself down there!) to the trenches."

just as for someone brought back with war wounds—I have trenches inside,
down to the depths, like a marrow transplant. it keeps getting deeper
while my spine tries to reject and expel it. in the guise of
feeling. a trench like any other, with the dead and wounded—thank god they're ours, at least!—,
(a finger drew them in the dust, but now that I'm carrying them inside,
someone pokes me with a finger to make sure they're real: *"fuck you!"*),
(about me they wrote that *in the trenches I hacked to pieces every bit of Nietzsche Goethe*
& Ko [. . .],
but it took poetry 70 years to catch up with me—as with *Lou[. . .] is*
nowhere.. . . .) as many times as I enter her, it's like the first time—all blood,
when I go out in the world with her, people ask me why I'm there with a common grave.
no doubt it's my blood, and no doubt it drags me to the very bottom!

wrinkles, the lifeline on my palm, stigmata, wounds—by whatever means, just bring her out into
the light of day,
stylets, drains, perfusions—anything, as long as I can expel it,
the glass urinal and the bedpan—as if you've got to empty the black sea with a thimble!
or fill it up—not even if two armies on the front line, both sides, squatted and
pissed into it like a latrine—, or abort it—damned birth,
no midwife can pull her out into the world. even Nietzsche's words cannot plumb that bottom!
it can't be seen, and not even vervain can help! such effort Nietzsche

to find out that I'm related by blood to a blade which gives birth—by a c-section—to
hemophiliac crown princes,
and that, up against the wall, my flesh flutters like a white flag: "don't shoot!"

(this is the end.) "fire!"—missa solemnis for me, the trenches

translated by
Adam J. Sorkin and Lidia Vianu

tanka

*"! as beautiful and perfect as Death at which everything
is ingathered under a cover, we yearn for the moment
when naked before us you are revealed in your radiance:
oh, the howl with which we cleaved you apart, Death,
oh, the blood on the lips of the primal hymen!"*
Cezar Ivănescu, "The Primal Virgin of Mankind"

unmatched in the nights when she spreads her legs, each more endless than the other,
          without beginning or end, like two world

wars—inscribed between them, those twenty-one years of his, when *he entered her*, the
          interwar

period, he cuts the exact measure of her gait, the line of the thigh, the *aery sprite* of the
          void between

her long gams, as if with his german *das ewig weibliche* he'd polish the french

pronunciation (*chercher la femme*)—a comparison that might have been inspired thanks to
          the birthmark

in the shape of a tank, on the inside of the calf, with its barrel pointing upward, aiming at
          her sex

(the story of a gesture: a hand applied to the belly of the young

math teacher in the middle of class when, cleaving it in two,

a column of soviet tanks had just entered the village, as if to

shield her pregnancy / the fetus kicking for the first time in the mother's turret of *cha(i)r* at
          the touch

of the one who, at the blackboard, a piece of chalk between her fingers—as if she herself
          daubed white with lime—explained: "two parallel lines

never intersect . . . ")

          a virgin, she swears *screw my mama's birth* / prays *blessed mary,*

mother of god. let her name be tanka, even though it's mary. in the name of the holy one,
          bear with grace

the two wars—the left one, with the *wari*cose vein!—through the heart of town, indifferent
                              to time's passing—the crosswalk a zebra of
white days and black days—under the sidelong fire in men's glances—her mother had
                              warned her: "whether cat
or man, you say scat at the entrance, or else you can't get rid of them"—, as if walking through
a minefield without a map, locked in her own shell—a tank-woman by birth—like a
                              goddess robed in breast-plates. ar-
more-d *oh, what a mama!* as light as if neither her mother had ever been heavy with her
nor the virgin mary with the One born not conceived (a love story: how
the void between the legs got hitched with their bare-naked master, as if *a match made*
in heaven).

                  history proceeds with a woman's gait: in '89, on the 7th of november, during
the military parade, bedded beneath the tanks beside the hundred more, taken on the
                              carriage by
the officer odysseus spending himself according to his (how many?) horsepower up to his
                              epaulettes: "this man treads, not fucks!";
raised up on her feet in '91, together with the state, a golem inscribed / traced with
a finger in the dust, befitting only the name: "(w)(o)rm"; so no one could see
the mark of the beast? the *warices*? on her legs, with boots of chernozem pulled high
above the eyes (*Requiescat in pace!*); on the roads (no road leads to rome
except *via* albania!) in recent last years; crouched
knees to mouth, as if rocking a pair of twins just torn away from the nipples.
in her power—conception; to his hands only writing has been granted.
and then only after he gets under her skin, it must be done in the tank
on the inside of the calf, he revs the engine, the pistons thrust, he shoots
aiming at her sex
                  (the poem of the immaculate conception tears itself
from the lips: "open me!")

translated by
Adam J. Sorkin and Diana Manole

*kali*graphic poem

"if I'd sew all my lovers head to foot, I could escape from the gulag on the white trail of their
                              flesh,"
I whispered one winter night in moscow—to screw my courage up!—in the ear of naked
transcendence (to be sure, she also had an everyday name, but in bed I enjoyed speaking
                         this way). nature demanded
transparency and sex—she had both at the same time and without even getting out from
                         under the blanket. her reply
came at once: "if I were to tie all my lovers head to foot, the electric field
generated would be enough to fence a gulag." we talked only made-up stuff, literature. we *eli*
                              e-
*li*berated ourselves of readings. solzhenitzin, shalamov, razgon, etc. I caressed
her *kali*graphic body, as I were tracing, split into copulative and subordinate clauses, a
                         complex sentence:
"she looked like her entire life she'd drawn fallen men—dragging them on her own
                         shadow—from the battlefield, and
that's why she was always *en retard* with a grammatical tense, a flaw
she transformed into a quality." I kept reading between the lines *moskovskie novosti*: the
                              naked king
stuffed the mouths of children starved for truth with dirt. tbilisi, baku, yerevan. "I'm going
                         to have a baby,
but don't give it a thought," she told me one day. "we'll have." I tried *to anchor her in place*.
                         parentheses
made their appearance in my texts as her pregnancy became noticeable. the style
was born through the not at all chance meeting on a operating
table between a black hole stretched open across time zones like an gentleman's umbrella
                         and a sewing
machine. yet, *the oxen of the sun* has already been written . . .

when suddenly you appeared along my way,
yes, you, perestroika! . . . the rest is literature. the cell walls inscribed by the "enemies of
         the people" awaiting their
execution—the photograph that made its way around the world—is mere literature: up
         above, first, sentences
reconstructed, each of them, a "life story" the same as in a DNA chain. *stalin has no*
         patience.
simple propositions of the "sentence per man" type; one meter lower, someone scratched
         only a name.
a bead-roll of the dead followed, names, then three fingers off the floor only initials. and no
         one has
ever for any reason broken that unwritten law of context! (the lesson
about the style has been assimilated after all those years, thus I too subscribe myself on the
         wall with graffiti:

em. g.-p.)

translated by
Adam J. Sorkin and Diana Manole

(po)em G(eo)-p(olitical)

"I felt the power of g"
Cesare Pavese, *This Business of Living*

"*Là j'ai touché le point sensible*"
Serge Gainsbourg, "Love on the Beat"

unruly alphabets grow between the thighs of girls during puberty—some curly, others
straight, as willed by god
(to each girl in bloom a culture of her own: from grapevine to sugarcane). and then, because
of the reproductive
instinct, the hand longs to write. to lick molasses from the fingers, at the lesson's end,
after you've caressed the curlicues of the vine's tendrils, that's what I'd call a treat—
as if you'd unroll a papyrus and as you laid it down it changed into a straw mat with a
concubine already on it!
there's no need to understand them as long as they themselves don't exactly know which one
they are and what language they belong to, but enjoy
how they lend themselves to being learnt by heart. in a sweet abandonment with the first to
show up. scolding him:
"if it's already written on the forehead, why is it still read on the palm—with the hand
sous les jupes des filles?! . . . " pubis ovidius na[so screwed] knows what's up!
not a grammar in heat but rather the lover's body as a practical lesson on geopolitics:
the parallels are in fact bra straps; the time difference, when—*with sleepy eyelids*—you dis-
robe one shoulder in astral time, in dream, and the second in your bed, in local time. and the
meridians? at one
with the elastic of the lover's panties, from her head to the hem of her dress in the northern
hemisphere,
as long as you looked at her upwards from underneath. and, since you lowered
—not your eyes, but your hand!—across the equator, into the southern hemisphere, there
you happen upon

her dark continent. so that it fades to black before your eyes, when she shows

her africa curls beneath the finger[tips, "it's not like I've been made tipsy with a finger!"]

a blonde negress reveals the alphabet to ion creangă's white slave harap alb, but only as far

as the letter *g*—it's not as if she were frigid, but she wants to reach her wedding night a
                    virgin—,

when she's just barely keeping it a *tabula rasa*—"'cause I'm pregnant and health standards
                    demand it"—the simple manual

ability turns into knowledge. the one who feeds on them is not the same person as

the one who grows them—she starts reciting the alphabet and he suddenly finds out
                    that he [himself] would have to assimilate the entire unabridged
                    dictionary.

if I'd have her, just one, wrapped around my little finger so I'd be all set! all of them good (in
                    bed)

and beautiful, in the most perfect of all possible worlds. the alphabets grow, bloom, bear
                    fruit—each according to the language of

whose they are—on their own, until they become belladonnas. you didn't even get, as you
                    were supposed to, to the indefatigable cyrillic,

in the eighties and, look at you with your mouth full of vulgata—the pronunciation still
                    leaves much to be desired!—

like a true product of the *sixties—années folles—*, such as "the G generation"

and *punctum* (while the west was starting to circulate "the ecstasy pill," moldovan

linguists made up, if I may say so, the miracle spot of the language, the letter Ж—

still a russian Ж, only now displaying gioconda's smile, on the face of жеоржета ивановна—;

and that was how you learned about G from elementary school on, in first grade, she in '68,
                    you in '71,

but not until two decades later, in moscow, you hers). the metaphysics of sex

avenged by genetic (*yin*)gineering, the handwriting (*yin*)genuous on the dot (on i, as in

inguinal) makes way for the writing, perverse (from the hair around the prick). and again

unruly alphabets grow between the thighs of girls during puberty—some curly, others
                    straight, as willed by . . . both this way

yet again that way: the alphabets grow, bloom, bear fruit—each according to the language of

whose—until they get to . . . full stop. now let's take it

from the top

translated by
Adam J. Sorkin and Diana Manole

the rosary

at one end of the swing—a wooden board balanced on springs—she, the skin, at the other,
                    he, the bones.
she the more exposed, he the more enclosed. she—plank—he. his
falling (trochee) / her return (iamb) break the space into poetic feet, choriambs,
where redskins, the dusk, rise up—along the horizon line the day's scalp /
while the swing freezes in the position of 10 minutes after 8
ut is the old name of the note *do. re* reflects in the mirror as *er. ut-er.* the *us* of the two astride
                    a piece
of lumber, each greeting the other halfway, bouncing in the saddle as if on springs, like racing
                    in a steeple-
chase, the skin and the bones—who above whom?—ride against each other. bone on bone.
                    from one line to
the next, the skin. he, she. as much as . . . , so much that . . . in the enjambment-swing, each
the other's counterweight. two poetics—in balance, the plank—set on the same scale.
she writes as if the skin, absorbing the atmosphere of hellas from the sky, would tan: nude;
                    from inside
out, like earth pushing one day to the surface a handful of sacred
relics—every little bone, curling around nothingness / the inward emptiness, is a papyrus
                    scroll from the *egyptian*
book of the dead—, the bones. the rocking on the swing, on the spot, the naked form of god's
                    mechanics—*the sky ascending /*
the sky descending—, and after the plank lowers him into the earth / it will thrust
her high into heaven, follow exactly the nature of each voice ascending / descending,
                    inscribed in the melodic profile of her phrase / in the bone structure of
                    the rosary
of her rhythm. the poem reveals itself in the shape of a woman / caught up with from behind,
remembrance of His shoulders balancing—*the via crucis*, on the streets of jerusalem—the
                    plank

that passes beyond, enlarging the perspective, into the horizon line, translucent, and on it
in a row

the sun at one end of the verse, at the other the moon. the sun, the moon

translated by
Adam J. Sorkin and Diana Manole

the poem of reflections

from hand (mine, in which he died) to mouth, his being became the (posthumous) calling of
                    his name:

zabolotsky is dead, my master, who was worth *n*[o less than all of the country of moldova's]
                    lei!

in vain I reach out my hand—shorter now by the death of a bird—after *what I had and*

lost, my gesture disappears beyond the horizon. and even were I

to chop it off at the wrist and set it in the cage in his place, it's not going to speak, not even in
                    sign

language—without words experience gains in intensity but loses in duration, the same way as
                    with the last breath you bequeath

приказал долго жить*—, yet, between the two of us, I'm the one about whom it was said:
                    "he's handy with the quill."

shrinking above the paper into *manipulation* [a calligraphy pen], the hand—as if I'd clasp
                    between my hands a bead-roll, so

asymmetrical is the life line on the left in comparison to what's read on the right—

transcribes an afternoon on the thirteenth, sunday—a gloomy day—, of a

talking parrot (so many refractions, his words: *birdchicken galaicost kissyplease skirtgenius*

cymbalrhymester)—with invisible ink I add: "of a poet"—preening his plumage in a little
                    mirror

which, of course, won't retain his reflection—the practice to inlay in the space where a photo
                    should

appear on the headstone, above/below the name of the one laid to rest, a little mirror wherein
a passerby would recognize himself, why does this come to mind?—, not even the semblance
(indelible) of the double—read in a mirror, the reflection of death is the same, looky-looky,
                    the spitting image of the inborn

---

* (Russian) literally: he wished us happy birthday; hence: to live and remember him.

reflex—, peerless. sunday's the elevator on which he ascends to heaven. this date
was left between the 13th and 14th [of january], of the new year [2002] in the old calendar.
from hand to mouth. in his mother tongue.

no angel in the kingdom
of heaven, no trace of birds—what's left of heaven after you subtract earth—from beneath the
clay shore
no *tuba mirum*: emptied of marrow, our bones one day become, in the archangels' orchestra,
the woodwinds:
for tuning—his; mine, likely, a slide trombone (femur & tibia pulled to hell and back),
to give voice to faraway lands, through which nothingness must trumpet *the kingdom,
and the power, and the glory*, so that—for one of us already in the past tense—
*a whirlwind and a motion sparked and bones began to draw near one another, each bone to its
joint*—a textual
graft, in this case, takes the place of the marrow of the spinal column: as on judgment day:

arise arise doomed little bones
treading with death upon death
from beneath the black nail of the moon
rises a sun half dark with earth

indulge yourself each day of your life and try
every pleasure of ripening flesh
now, *despite our times*; later, stymied by worms . . . eternity
lasts no longer than a sunset's blush

you'll soon learn braille with tight-shut eyes
on a night with no way to cross the sky's shallow wash
and bones again in the belly . . . get thee to paradise!
the party invites us from the bane of hell's wish-

bone. arpeggios follow in [*dies*] su*ir*[*a*]*e*. what if I were to imagine arranging the dear little
                              bones side by side—like the many rungs
of a white ladder—, *a stairway to heaven?* it's no big deal, unless flesh goes back down to
                              earth [*yeah, may you bleach as bare bones*], to follow him to
the heights? his death, I had it in my hand. when I write, the cemetery
crawls on its belly through the dust to eat out of my palm. that's it. the separation
rips apart—making a fair share for each—a common memory: during the black-and-white
days, in the winter of the year 2000, when throughout the entire territory of the republic of
                              moldova there were power cut-offs—said to be "fanning out"—
from the source of energy (*alias*, the light in the east), chișinău being—this time, truly—
ch-ău, deep chaos, on one of the evenings—and they seemed endless, like imperfect
                              verbs—it happened
that it surprised him in flight, the blackout. I kept track of him by ear—sound reflections—
                              crashing
into the walls like a feathered shuttlecock tossed into a strange court. groping,
I reached out to him, putting on darkness—a photographer's sleeves—up to my elbows,
                              eventually happening upon a box
of matches that he himself had dropped to the floor a while ago, and the stump of a candle.
                              the light
surprised us searching, each for one another, with shadows . . .

translated by
Adam J. Sorkin and Diana Manole

a meter of vodka cubed

honoring the memory of ioan flora

when we became blood brothers, flora and I, instead of trading shirts, as is customary, we
                traded passports:

yugoslav for soviet—at that time, both the one and the other from countries that no longer
                existed, but to which we had to return

after "the days of blaga" poetry festival in cluj-alba-iulia. he back to belgrade / I to the
                chaos of chișinău, each under the other's name, thus sheltered from

nato bombing/russian artillery. "*the postman*," we laughed with one voice, "*always rings
                twice.*"

(as if death arrives in the mail and if it doesn't find the addressee, it gets returned to the
                sender and won't wait for you

in post restante). after which we pledged brotherhood. a shot. arms intertwined so as to
                pretend we're communicating vessels.

"*pour, bro!*" then I did. then he did. then we did. *an accursed people!* breaking with a wave
                upon water the first circle enlarged the glass's mouth; the two of us

were on the same wavelength. and to complete our brotherhood, he said: "hey, let me tell
                you how my fellow serbs drink.

one enters a bar and orders a meter of vodka, which the barman pours—by eye!—directly
                on the bar

polished by the elbows of those who didn't feel lazy, a stream the length of a forearm plus a
                hand, exactly. the *ethanol standard* the joint's been called

ever since. and your russians? . . . " "they do it by ear!" and I told him how any russian is
                able—

just by ear!—to pour into 0.2 l.-glasses, cut into numerous facets, a bottle of vodka neatly
                in three.

                         ah! țuică is drunk and *alcohol* written!

in turn a few and then a few more passed away down the glass's mouth to fulfill (done by
                Thy will!) *the circle of poets*

who are gone: the ones left here roll the shot glasses in their hand as if tuning in the
wavelength. by spirits and tumblers.

while together with alcohol fumes an ethylic elite of poets also rises to the skies—mady,
emil, ioan (the list remains open)—like an aurora

borealis that burns with a blue flame, while our days more and more resemble white
nights. from young owls

we turned unexpectedly into mourning nightingales, according to how many companions
(of the writing desk)

with no warning we had to hold all-night wakes for. just as, having partaken of a cure,

you don't even know, since then, how you've fallen back into drinking again, the ante-
humous

turns itself into posthumous. dust to earth. and the glass up to the mouth. along the circle.
not the dead man

up from the grave. it'd be useless to mourn him—regrets are the burps of the spirit!—;
they've no way to turn into brine, no matter how salty

they can be, the tears. rather clearing our throats we should tell, in two voices (vitalie and
I), about the deed—similar to

a feat of arms, with the sole difference that it wasn't blood that flowed but vodka—of some
soldiers in the soviet army

caught in the barracks with a crate of vodka, who had the drink confiscated, the bottles
locked in the safe.

thus, alas, before becoming the one-night bride of the soldiers, vodka was (to remain) an
iron virgin.

sing, o muse, of the night assault of a platoon of russian soldiers on a battery of bottles,
their strength cubed.

how they took the safe in their arms, how they shook it—in their desire to get sloshed—
like caragiale's drunken citizen.

how they achieved the great break-in, an inside job, in the sense that they smashed the
bottles into pieces. how, filtered

through a pillowcase turned inside out, the alcohol filled the washbasin to the brim
("vodka up the wazoo!
I never thought I'd learn to drink vodka by the basinful . . . "). how, towards morning, the
barracks were dreaming of
l'eau-de-vie en rose. how, upon waking, many of them threw up in the basin from which
they drank. how they were forced to run drills
all day, with gas masks on their faces, so that—"алкоголь, выходи! никотин, выходи!"*—
alas, instead of making them feel better,
they got dizzy . . . protect us, god, from premature ejaculation and *esprit de l'escalier!*

what a great brotherhood could've been if the meter of vodka (of flora) had been cubed (by
me), on the spot.
if the earth were transparent (as in blaga's poem), surely we'd have made a toast, just as the
air gets cut into facets. such a drinking
buddy I had in my life—his death turned me upside-down like a shot glass.
(open parentheses: december 1950—
close parentheses, february 2005.)
as long as the horizon is the mouth of the glass. *is no one*
pouring now, bro?

translated by
Adam J. Sorkin and Diana Manole

---

* (Russian) "alcohol, get thee gone! nicotine, get thee gone!"

self-portrait with eyeglasses of tea

with a skeleton arm, munch. with his ear cut off, van gogh. self-portrait with an eye put
                    out, victor brauner . . . death
like a canvas of groundwater in a picture frame of bone, with a ground of flesh, on an easel
                    of mourning, appears to size me up
as I search its gaze/as it studies me: "what's up?"
                    39.
(a temperature? years? eminescu's age at death?) a subtraction of being when you shake
the thermometer. at the other end of the gesture, the hand pouring into glasses statues of
                    black women in *lipton*
yellow label tea. little glass stalls, these tea goblets, in which my black women take a shower.
                    and I can see
in each 2-g. *quality no. 1* teabag, a pregnancy: *all with twins, and not a one of them infertile.*
each one in the flow of her own waterfall, long tresses hanging heavy down their backs,
                    from head to toe. and I,
a (thinking) cane of sugar, reflected in a virgin's eye out of which
soars a rainbow into the other eye like the arc of a pince-nez. tea with milk, the virgin.
a stripe of black-ink, the rainbow. this death,
her eyes—two shot glasses of cognac tossed over her head
together—the color of theine, batting their lashes as if snapping fingers in anger:
                    "what'll you do to her? . . . "
to see her—I shouldn't cast an eye on her!—I've put on my eyeglasses of tea. don't look at
how I'm lying on the floor, eyes on the ceiling—and the spine's chainsaw sets to its task,
                    cutting
into the living flesh birch forests as tall as a man, the blood's sawmill
splits them into hand's-width planks on which, at the hour of the evening service,
the *toaca* is drummed loud and fast for the prayer to jesus, uttered by the heart—and
                    revealed to you is a landscape

84

framed in the box of your eyelids, with a man, dying for women since he was a little child
                        in the first edition/
books with the shoulders of mannequins that change their bandages
with infusions evening after evening as if flayed of what he fucked with his gaze/read all
                        day long.
a man, as has been shown, whose protein has apparently been replaced by theine.

you'll only see an apparition, inside four walls, polished
by readings—every proofed page turns into sandpaper—a shadow thrown
(by ideas?) on the asphalt that, no matter what you do, you can't make
more comfortable in its chalk outline; no more than a projection
in aeternum, in black and white, deaf to *verweile doch, du bist so schön!**

a mirror wearing a black veil (of tea) wandering through
a strange abrasive landscape
on joplin's soundtrack:

> No, no, no, no, no, no, no, no, no, no, no, no, no, no, no, no
> No, no, no, no, no, no, no, no, no, no, no, no, no, no, no, no
> No, no, no, no, no, no, no, no, no,
> Don't you cry,
> Cry.

freeze-frame

        on the branch of the gesture, flesh and blood like a charm hanging from
a tree on the last day of march 2003—when the poet and woman dies on poetry day—
a charm my mother wore on her bosom (I'm summoning up
my own self-portrait, writing about my dear shadows—

---

* (German) Oh, stay, you're so beautiful!—Goethe, *Faust*, II, act 5.

aurel, cristian, ioan horațiu, iustin, mariana—just like

the renaissance painter who painted his subjects sitting at night by the flame

of candles stuck firmly in his hat—a true candelabrum—which he took off

his head only to replace burned-out candles, the price

of the light—just that!—being the value of his painting. so to speak, the burning

of everything enters into the price of things. namely, at thirteen, eight, six, two, several
                                        months
of light-years—and the calculation isn't yet complete—

since the passing on of aurel, cristian, ioan horațiu, iustin, mariana,

I write in the line of the extinguished, I, calligrapher of shadows), hanging below her heart.

I came   · I saw   I closed
my eyes tight

(under your eyelids, a black woman with blue blood—your vision—puts on her widow's
                        black weeds)

translated by
Adam J. Sorkin and Claudia Serea

brother emil

if you don't have a hanged brother emil, like rebreanu, it's useless to try to write prose.
better than a plumb bob on a string is the brother's noose, for a boost in precision.
a grandfather clock requires winding yet it still falls behind now and then, while for
              brother emil
the cuckoo clock struck right at the hour. especially if you write a novel
there's no way you can do without a brother emil swinging from the gallows for high
              treason—
all the higher as his brother's deed, not to shoot those of his own blood, is more debasing.
there's no replacement for a brotheremil, no matter how many classes of lieutenants
              graduate from military
schools from this day on. if you've a brother, you've a book!—the history of romanian
              literature bears witness.
as many dear spirits hang around, that's how many kibitzers. you play, in your brother's
              name, the hanged man
card, and the writing desk frolics under your elbows, just like the stool under
brother emil's feet—a world in suspense.

                                    no one should dare sit at the writing table—
dissection table, wake table, it's all the same—who doesn't have a brother emil, a suicide,
like mircea ivănescu's—, one day later than he decided to (because *that* evening
he couldn't miss a concert!). poetry is someone else, a being departed before its time who
              gets
continued in the lines of those who remain—in their own image—, growing old together.
from *the other*, not from himself, the poet sets forth, the same as with the serial suicide
              "through predecessors."
if god hasn't given you a brother emil, don't let poetry cross your mind!
better than the silencer installed on the gun barrel is his young temple,
when it pushes you towards writing cerebral poems—and what a relief that *the hand that*

writes isn't what must place the full stop, pulling the trigger! all your life to feel guilty
about that, even if you have no guilt, ends up usurping the role of self-consciousness.

a name predestined to fit you like a glove—don't confuse their hands!—the hanged man's &
        the suicide's.
take the hand now of one, then of the other—don't confuse their names!—brother emil, the
        first
who's as much lacking as the second one's absent, and who scheduled a meeting on your
        chest
like two post-mortem medals, in the rank of knight (of the sorrowful countenance). an
        officer in the reserves,
you play orderly now to one—"line up!"—then to the other—"at ease!"—, the same
eternal lieutenant. it's simply that there's no one—unless you're your own brother emil to
        yourself—to take his place.
let yourself be written by brotheremil, *in absentia*, before brotheremil gives up writing,
only so that in the end even you can make—good, bad—a name for yourself! (now, in first
        person:
I'm brotheremil, the hanged man & the suicide of tomorrow. playing games,
I lost my life at cards. at reading cards. at writing cards, my life.)
names are all as if from the dead—given gratuitously, when there's no one to call you:
        mon em.

translated by
Adam J. Sorkin and Diana Manole

(Diaphragm)

A Character in Repose

1. "I'm dy-y-ing," he barely whispered coming back to himself, though frightened by what he'd said, he immediately covered his mouth with his hand,

2. but too late, for his voice passed through the hole in the middle of his hand and whirling in a spiral into the air, in ever wider circles, emptied the space around him: "I'm dy-y-ing!"

3. That he wouldn't see how they move out of sight, houses, living beasts and human beings—here or there towards anywhere or nowhere—

4. leaving him in an absolute void, he covered his eyes with his hand,

5. but too late, for his gaze passed through the holes in the middle of his hands and, splitting itself in two,

6. it had had more than enough and ran away, going wherever the eyes led it.

7. He lay back motionless, propped up, his hands open towards the sky, feeling how through their middle the lines of life and fate and, drop by drop, the sweat, leaked away.

8. "From now on, no one will read my palm," he thought and his thought leaked out through the hole in one of his hands.

9. To hide his wounds, they tried to wrap them in bandages, like a mummy, but the bandages leaked through the holes in his hands, and people's fingers, probing the wounds—to check on them!— leaked the same way, enlarging the holes.

10. His robes, from the sleeves to the hem, likewise leaked through the holes in his hands, chafing them with their knots and seams, enlarging them.

11. His shoes also leaked, dusty and worn to nothing along with the roads they traveled.

12. And the nails which fastened him in place leaked through his open, blind hands, piercing them.

13. The stable where he was born leaked away through the holes in his hands, together with the cattle and the star above, along with the

magi who came to worship him and the children slain in his stead.

14. He picked up sand in one hand and the sand leaked through the hole in his hand. He tried to heap it up in the other hand, but it leaked from this one too. "It all just runs through my hands!" he whispered.

15. He lay motionless, bemoaning his bones, his hands open towards the sky, feeling how his appearance kept leaking through the holes in his hands: a first impression at the beginning, his true face a little later, his air of absentmindedness, and, at the end, his secret face, open towards mysteries.

16. From his arms and legs his gestures leaked out, then, like big rivers during the drought, his arms and legs.

17. Everything he'd ever embraced and on which he'd laid his hands leaked through the holes in his hands.

18. What good luck for axial symmetry, otherwise the lungs, kidneys, heart, liver, solar plexus, etc., etc. would have rushed together to leak through a single hole and, God forbid! might have got stuck somewhere, clogging their passing.

19. Only the brain, obstinate as usual, couldn't decide for a long time which hole it should leak out through, seeking every argument pro and con for each of them.

20. His entire bloodline, the living and the dead, leaked through the holes in the hands: his mother's relatives—through the heart's side, his father's—through the right.

21. Everything around him started spinning, ecstatically, becoming the light and music of the spheres, but even this music leaked out through his hands with a hole in the middle, like two separate sides of the same phonograph record, although it's hard to imagine how the sides of the same record can be separated.

22. Time itself leaked out through the holes in the hands, without healing his wounds.

23. "What a perfect hourglass!" he thought as the last lines and features leaked through the hands drew together in another dimension, forming the very same hand.

24. "From now on my hands will be the tablets of the law," his ideas leaked out through the holes in his hands and coagulated, gathering itself in another dimension.

25. "What good luck for axial symmetry," he then thought, "or else how could they have crucified me if I'd only one hand?"

26. The bandages, as well as his clothes and shoes, leaked into another dimension, returned to the body leaked into another dimension.

27. Everything he had embraced and laid his hands on, having leaked through the holes in his hands, gathered in another dimension.

28. His entire bloodline, the living and the dead, having leaked through the holes in the hands, reappeared in another dimension: his mother's relatives—on the heart's side, his father's—on the right.

29. The world itself, having leaked through the holes in his hands, became transfigured, gaining another dimension; time itself, after it leaked through the holes in his hands, was transfigured, without healing his wounds.

30. He picked up sand in one hand and the sand leaked through the hole in his hand into another dimension. He tried to heap it up in the hand from another dimension but it leaked from there too into his hand from former times.

31. "It all just runs through my hands!" he whispered, though frightened by what he'd said, he immediately covered his mouth with his hand . . .

32. " . . . through my hands, but generous: *Come, eat . . . !*" and frightened by the seen and the unseen, he covered his eyes with his hands . . .

33. " . . . but the world knew Him not"

translated by
Adam J. Sorkin and Diana Manole

II. *Seven Poems*

Gestures

I. *(alpha and omega)*

I feel the shape of the hand opening my body's
perfect gesture—for as long as
a gesture lasts. I feel the shape of His hand
setting free the alphabet: aleph
in the sacred ox, beta in the poor
living beast . . .
                      and then after they
had come into being—each separately
and all at once: "I feel the shape of His hand
perfect in the gesture of completing
the hooves or the horns or the tail"—
I alone wanted not to be mere gesture
even if of His hand. like the blind man
I felt the working of His hand
naming them, I prayed for the toothed
shell of the mouth out of which came forth
the soft tongue of the snail who since
that moment has carried me on his back. the road
of *speech* I articulated: along it
I led by hand—Your hand following, in gestures
leaving forever other shapes—the animals
in the pastures: thus aleph
gesticulating fulfilled itself in omega.
above them I trembled: in small, tentative
gestures dispersing the shape of His hand . . .

. . . by my fingertips I might still
hang on, nothing more than I am

a gesture taking His body down from the cross

2. *(Pieta)*

from high to low—as you'd lower
a flag: the folds of flesh
into the folds of her lap   the wax
model of the final gesture into the gesture
of welcome   the body under eyelids fixed
wide open in her vigil   the freefall
in the gravity of the gesture with which
from right to left the sign of the cross
ends in the heart—*mater mater*

matter enfolded into thought

3. *(the transfiguration)*

a gesture per second publicly renounces the body
without pain   eventually the final gesture
will forsake him without regret   translucent
throughout the city there wander a multitude of gestures
filled by opaque bodies for an instant, emerging
from them transfigured   your own gesture

takes form that you sometimes fill there   *and* then
all you can say is: "this instant I once lived"
until one day face to face you
bump up against the being into whom
gesture by gesture you transferred freedom   the being from which
another body peels away at each gesture   *in* each body
with disgust you recognize yourself

4. *(Job)*

upon the weak flesh left behind all at once
the wandering gestures return with great pomp:
some gestures are the mourners   some
gestures come to scatter his ashes upon his head
to tear the hair from His head   some
gestures to break his hands—that he can
no longer break bread   some gestures to set
free the slaves in his body   some gestures
to throw him through a gesture into one final
gesture extended like a hand beg-
ging for the spare silver coins of
a few gestures of pity

5. *(foreign body)*

I head out into the city—to be alone—but I get snared in the sign language of the deaf
without meaning to: suddenly I find myself between two deaf

men on the crowded tram, caught between their words like a helpless insect
in a net. around their necks they wear small crosses: likely when
they shake their heads too vigorously, the crosses
run down their backs. but most of all by the way they tie off
the ends of their words, they resemble two spiders—from their shoulders
gestures grow continuously, as though each of them conjugates
his arms in the imperfect according to different grammatical
rules, with the morphology of bones and cartilage, an entire
vocabulary imprinted on one hand—a sort of mendeleev table
(I, for one, when I splash water on my face to keep from falling asleep in this poem, I feel
my facial bones
with my hands, but I don't see the old-hag grin), with the syntax
of three-dimensional space compensating
for the lack of phonetics (the conductor's hands, which are
the keystone of music, only they too know this syntax).
I ride the tram, captive in their words—a foreign body—transparent
like a lab animal escaped from its cage that arrives by chance
in the schematics of a new testing machine a day before
the experiment. meanwhile words get woven
with words. I'm afraid, as I keep tossing around, that I'll break the threads. that I'll tangle
the strands. but I realize I'm still stranger to them than
the totemic rock of a caveman, the rock through which
daughter-in-law could talk to father-in-law. I—a foreign body—
snagged in the words of a pair of mimetic silences: before being and after.
gestures of divine marionettes (see craig's postulate: "man—the creature of nature—
is a foreign body in the abstract structure of the work of
art." and what is the sign language of the deaf if not
pure lyric poetry?!). in the city of iași, on the crowded tram, I had the revelation
of god's hands—not molded, but alive—, sliced off by
a winter sunrise, the gleaming knife of the celes-
tial guillotine: the two deaf men, each abandoning his

sleeve of darkness, communicated with one another. in the meantime tangled
within their dialogue, I didn't get off the tram until the very last
stop, feeling physically how I was becoming
less and less a foreign body, more and more of a body in common with the silence
before being and after
gesture

6. *(living tissue)*

describe how the puppeteer, before fitting the puppets on his fingers, would weigh his
                              hands in turn
—one like a bony loach, the other soft, they complement each other as in the quotation
from miron costin: *where there's space to linger, linger more, where there's need*
to keep it short, shorten it more—, how, after the show,
he'd lay his hands, more dead than alive, on the cold pans of a balance with the sheen of a
                              dissection
table: my art has the exact weight I lose making art,
his hands stripped of gestures would express, withdrawn
from the puppets—without them, now simple sleeves each sewn at one end—as if being
                              born.
describe, sir, how he'd wash his hands after weighing them describe how he'd
abandon the characters, still living, of pepi
and pepita—she, as it has been said, *where there's space to linger, linger more,* and he, in
                              turn, *where*
there's need to keep it short, shorten it more—, how behind his back he'd hide their
nakedness after sinning, self-conscious, as in Genesis 3:10, how he'd slip his hands into his
                              pockets like letters
without stamps or addresses into the mailbox: after us there remains (at best) only
                              messages in the dead-letter office.

describe how, after the show, the puppets wouldn't
peel off his hands, how they'd get under his skin in his life and work
as a puppeteer (up to his elbows in the puppets, like a midwife), how, half born, they'd
                              make
a common body—half in the grave—with his own
being, now—so that the nothingness won't swallow it—hanging with both
hands onto their tongues: *where there's space to linger, linger more, when there's*
need to keep it short, shorten it more, they said in the characters' three voices when

god put my arms on the page, like two witnesses: adam and lilith

how can I write, I shouted at him, when I'm ureche the chronicler, but my hands answer to
misaile the monk and simioane known as the church cantor

7. *(the bead-roll)*

I feel the shape of the hand opening my body's
perfect gesture so slowly
so patiently that I complete
the tally of my age in the time the gesture takes
spreading my arms wide to both sides
—fulfilled at 33 years old—
as the moustache turns gray as
the blackberry of the eye ripens as the milk
of His face rises
to foam over into the stove's flame as all this
is surely enough to mourn having
a mother sweet mother as you'd be

my lover opening from the depths
of your being the gestures of our daughter—dragoşă
and rareşă—as praying deeply
I'd open up with letter-gestures
His perfect hand that in anger
would anxiously shake all my small gestures
out of my limbs: as
there'd remain enough for me to be myself
and for what remains not to remain
enkidu, but the gestures in which
I'd mourn his being so as to prolong
my being in a cry like a deaf-mute's
through gestures—*"the I of my own I"*—
I feel the shape of His hand closed within the
perfect gesture of the body . . .
to be ended . . .
amen

translated by
Adam J. Sorkin and Diana Manole

The Beaten-Carries-the-Unbeaten

(*initial version*)

Motto: "Better than to walk is to stand on your feet, better than to stand on your feet is to sit, better than to sit is to lie down, better than to lie down is to sleep, better than to sleep is to die, better than to die is never to have been born"

(indian saying)

I

I'm my own brother *cainabel*: there's no one lonelier than he, he-with-
an-eye-of-blood-with-one-of-fire-the-eye-of-blood-extinguishinging-the-eye-of-fire
lamenting to himself: "I no longer have a brother!" in his arms he carries
his brother's shadow bunched up like a bed sheet
just now tossed aside the heat of the human being still re-
tained in folds of semi-darkness   I'm my own brother *cainabel*
rocking my brother's shadow in my arms: "*hush, little baby,*
hush-up or else . . . " and in the morning sun
open wounds appear pleats in the shadow
ragged at the edges of the wretched brother   I'm my own brother *cainabel*
running from light's scythe with an ever paler face
whistling past his heels his brother's
shadow shrinking from his hands towards noon:
he had but one single day of light to mourn him to carry
his shadow in his arms—"*hush, baby, hush-up or else . . . "—at the setting*
of the sun shadows flee withdraw then vanish into the dark
world of shades and . . .   I'm my own brother *cainabel*
struggling with my brother's shadow as it grows heavier towards evening
lamenting to himself: "I no longer have a brother!" in his arms he can barely carry
his brother's shadow which grows slips out of his hands floods

the ground that he runs across stepping on

his brother's shadow which keeps growing he trips on it falls

gets up again runs across the beloved shadow

towards sunset . . .   crushed underfoot

his brother's shadow keeps spreading until it catches up with the night

of the wake when the final parting will be decided . . .

stained light of sunset: only a moment

together with the shade I'm my own brother *cainabel:* there's no one lonelier than he, he-
with-

an-eye-of-water-with-one-of-fire-the-eye-of-water-extinguishing-the-eye-of-fire

III

"I'm you you're me: which of us is dying?"
(I come

upon you   you speed through me like a cannonball I've no time

to stand aside because I'm filled with you

while my blood grows claws: with them I ransack

your entrails so I don't feel you

scratch every segment of my spinal column

with a nail: I'm you you're me   each

caught in a net of the other's blood   you're

my ego's obsession you're my headache

I'm your puke the bloody foot

sticking its phalanges into your balls gripping

your future in my hands   and once again: I'm you you're me)

who keeps shouting and who keeps answering:

"instead of my mama crying, much better your mama crying!"

"I'm me you're you: who will rise from the dead?"
(against my will

I draw the dagger from the skin scabbard of your arm
you pluck the hurtling arrow of your blood from
my heart's quiver   we exchange prisoners
with "mine" for "yours"   it won't do
to fill my being with "me" since exactly that much
was you   when I see you deflated I suppose you
feel empty inside   ah! the purity
of the race! . . .   with a tight-fisted hand I pick
my children out of your balls   while you
grab your dolls and are gone)   each is
the absence of the other who shouts:
"instead of my mama crying, much better your mama crying!"

V

leaping so high for the bait that
he fell like a sack upon his shoulders
his legs for the first time detached from
his feet so suddenly free that
they hung dangling from his chest
over his body below from which he
leapt so high that he fell
like a sack upon his shoulders

the spine of the one who leapt
so high seems a slender stem
shooting out from the taut bow
of the vertebral column of the body below
from which he leapt
so high that he fell like a sack
upon his shoulders with the bait between his teeth

leaping for the bait eyes closed
falling back onto his shoulders the-one-above
has no eyes at all he forgot them
on the face of the body below from which
he leapt so high that he fell
onto himself on his shoulders like a sack

he has the point of view of
the-one-below (he has no eyes to see him!)
and so that he'll never accidentally lose him
he doesn't climb down from his back that's why
he pees himself on the-one-below from whom
he leapt so high that he fell
like a sack upon his shoulders

he doesn't walk down below with his feet on the ground
in the pockets of the-one-below with his hands
dropped into the hands of the-one-below when the-one-
below secretly prays to the One-
Above: "descend upon me God
I'll carry you I'm the one from whom
I leapt so high that I fell
upon my shoulders . . . "
                    in this way
years pass he becomes very much heavier
(how had he been able to leap so
high that he fell onto himself upon his shoulders?)
retired he composes poems:
"I'm levitation itself above
this abyss of a body from which

I leapt so high that I fell
like a shade upon my shoulders"

now every day there grows inside him
(here and there) a coffin of
oak he concludes the bait was
an acorn which he purposely dropped
above him the round pink snout
of the strangers' sun (the poet has
once seen it "*cou coupé*")
                              "above
all of the above!"—tells himself the one that upon himself
onto the shoulders fell the one who is
a hump on his own—"where your head is
your feet must needs be!"

VII

The Beaten-carries-the-Unbeaten tells him stories to kill time:
" . . . and when the Unbeaten
tires of walking on my back he takes my left hand
carefully looks at it from above and blowing
the web of lines from my palm into the wind
lightly as if a spider web
he catches it with long fingers
nimble as knitting needles ties it by himself
between two slender stems—swinging as in a hammock in
the lines from my palm—always untying it always having
to move it into the shadows always between two
magnetic poles two breasts two acacia trees between two
monuments—like in a hammock swinging—between

a pair of forgotten crutches two linden trees two oases

two swords thrust into the hot sands of the Desert

two tongues that praising him ceaselessly swing him

like a shah between two women between two

continents (how frayed and worn

the web of lines from my palm gets!) always between two

doubts between two legs (mine) in this way hobbling me

like a horse—so I can't run!—between two

viziers two slaves two days

swinging in the web of lines as in a hammock

with his women with the eunuchs the cold weapons:

he's cruel and unjust but no matter what I do he never

beats me on the palm of my hand with a ruler

and so never breaks the resilient thread—he doesn't know it's the lifeline—that

he always ties between two columns

between two camels two border markers

two knees of the woman he loves who gives birth

to his princely heir between

two crosses with our names—*the same*—carved in stone"

IX

"you'll meet the Bogeyman—the hay-*stuffed* felt field jacket

with a private's / general(*issimus*)'s insignia

on crossed sticks: present arms!"

every day

handsome men and women march before him—the parade

doesn't end not even when (tattered by the wind?!) the Bogeyman

suddenly stretches out his arms—from his armpits

two bats take off—and with

his empty sleeve he points amidst the motley crowd

at a random anybody: at the same time he's caught / she's caught naked /
stark naked she's driven / he's seduced to yield himself / herself to the Bogeyman
buttoned up to the top button: through one sleeve
there goes in through the other goes out
the victim's soul the body remains behind (throbbing
on two crossed sticks just like a transplanted
heart) to feed the jacket's
circulatory system: suddenly a red vein
appears on the epaulettes and pulses across them
until a second a third appear all three making
one thick vein that crosses lengthwise from end to end—then
suddenly it snaps!
                  and you barely
can take notice when the stars on the epaulettes
start swelling again until they reach the size of
the buttons the stars of a maréchal
until a ruby / vampire star rises on the rim of the kettle
serving the Bogeyman as a combat helmet . . .
the parade continues forever: lost in the crowd
The-Beaten-carries-the-Unbeaten and listens to his
tongue swollen—like a leech—with blood and jabbering:
"you'll meet the Bogeyman—present arms!"

XI

three-brothers-mounted-piggyback-on-one-another look they're coming this way
(not because the path's too narrow or the traffic's
too heavy—how could that be, here?—but the three
have only one suit of clothes and they wear it
at the same time: when the top one pulls the cap down on his forehead the second
girds himself in a long coarse peasant coat and the third

tugs his homespun pants up and it's let's go! . . .   so they walked and walked
until the one in the coat to keep from getting frostbite on his numb feet started
spurring the one below: "giddyap, little horsey, giddyap!" until the one
with the cap to keep his hands from shivering quickly plunged them
in the ears of the one in the middle . . .   so they walked and walked
the Beaten driving the Unbeaten hard and feeling under his heels
the rough tongue of the land the one riding
touching with his sensitive foot soles—two tongues, no less!—the little stones
in the poor man's guts with the vague sense that he'd walked
on a country road with the one with the cap twisting
the mind of the one underneath like a rubik's cube . . .   so they walked and walked
and they're still walking today if they haven't stopped somewhere: one deep blue from
cold another yellow as beeswax the last burning like a flame
the wind blows on them and frays them like a flag)   the middle one
has a hole—big enough to squeeze your head through—in his chest
and shout at the top of your lungs through your mouth and two nostrils:

"stop feeling dread   "we can't go home!   "olé! olé! oléééé!
communism's dead!"   the dead make us roam!"   ceaușescu's gone away!"

three-shivering-brothers-piggyback-on-one-another go to hell ass to head
(not because the path's too narrow or the traffic's
too heavy—how could that be, here?—but they haven't
a rag on them: the top one mounted on the middle one
the middle one on the bottom one who has no one to mount so that after seeing them
prudish presidents call out: tramps! . . .   and they carried
each other in turn on their backs bludgeoned by the miners harassed by the crowd:
"the-Beaten-carries-the-Unbeaten!" until they had nowhere to go
until look they come back exactly where they left in december—one's
deep blue from cold another yellow as beeswax the last burning with a flame
the wind blows on them and frays them like a flag)—in the chest

and you shout at the top of your lungs:

"…….…………….   "we can't go home!   "…….…………….
…….…………...!"   the dead make us roam!"   …….…..……...!"

XIII

       high above and even higher
       the alabaster of a monk's cell
from where with their hands full climb down six men down the steps
on each side of the dead: the evening's quiet
what a dis[arrangement] it is! an insect with wooden wings ingrown the coffin climbs down
with twelve pairs of legs on the steps of the inside (de)creasing stair-
case of the Khrushchev-style building
so narrow that the six men
to the coffin's left climbing down only one floor rubbed
their mourning ribbons against the whitewash on the wall like a
cataract on the eyes (of his bones à la *Modigliani*
even those alive can scarcely squeeze through this labyrinth!)
with the casket on their shoulders like a gigantic epaulette without insignias
the cortège in no way can fit on the landing
narrower than a passageway at customs (. . .)   suddenly a voice is heard:
       "open the door, christian
       open the door, christian . . . "
and suddenly the doors they felt the density of the wall with their shoulder blades: the dead still
on their shoulders the procession turns the corner entering up to the ankles the waist the arm-
pits of the dead man into the narrow vestibule where for a moment the masters
see themselves mirrored in the patent leather shoes of the deceased
just when he decreases from the armpits to the ankles in their household
space so that you can enter through the neighbor's
door headfirst as if he'd just come

into the world only to abandon it through the door

at the other equally narrow end of the landing where

they turn the corner (. . .)   *go slow with the coffin on the stairs!*

the cortège climbs down by entering at every tenant taking

the dead man out of their homes like a relative (. . .)   some bachelor apartment

they passed by long before jumps ahead squeezes itself

into the (his) reversed counting one and the others (. . .)   again from

        high above and even higher

        out of the alabaster of a monk's cell

the coffin with twelve pairs of legs climbs down the steps

of the spiral staircase cut in facets and nobody

notices that the air behind the windows is black that in the window's glass

moles are knocking earthworms not butterflies that the dead has put on

a monocle a square meter of darkness through which

he winks at us (. . .)   day night day the squaring

of the circle (. . .)   oh lord! if you knew what I saw through the monocle:

      . . . .

      an eclipse, a circumcised sun

translated by
Adam J. Sorkin and Diana Manole

The-Beaten-Carries-the-Unbeaten
(*revised and dehydrated edition*)

Motto: *"Mama's dearie, when I think of you*
I'm really glad yet feel so blue"
(funeral song from Hunedoara)

2

the caravan passed through the *eye* of *the needle—the gate of* our kingdom Gherghef
when the Infanta fell asleep with the kingdom in her lap
bewildered by sleep she forgot the pattern and embroidered with the silk road:
the devil May-he-go-to-the-desert has returned from the desert

the white day of our kingdom like linen stretched on hoops
became oily (who also wiped his face full of sweat with it?)
when the Infanta embroidered as you'd sew shut the mouth of a burlap flour sack:
May-he-go-to-the-desert has returned from the desert

like a thousand and one nights the suitors were ushered in pining away with longing
none of them could *thread the needle—*the portal to her chastity—sleepless the Infanta
wandered through the salons only her steps made sense:
May-he-go-to-the-desert has returned from the desert

her father married Fata Morgana on a Friday—since then the evil Stepmother
walks around and around her if only she'd drop from her hands the oasis Gherghef
the chambermaid whispered: "of all that the Infanta embroiders in a day there remains
only
May-he-go-to-the-desert has returned from the desert"

she gouged out her eyes with a needle—with her pricked fingertips
she searched feverishly for a way out (on every doorknob—blood):
"I embroidered the Empire with red thread I'll also unravel it where
May-he-go-to-the-desert has returned from the desert"

the caravan passed through the *eye* of *the needle—the gate of* our kingdom Gherghef
athletic slaves unload huge crates in front of the palace
"May-he-go-to-the desert returned in the bales of fabric the Desert
where he was exiled"—the Infanta wails at the top of her voice while

a young page has her on sacks stuffed full of sand

4

But look there comes the day when she also arms her slaves . . .
"order that the blasphemers be brought here! command the executioner
to pull out the tongue of each of them and . . . "—the boyar
kept on whispering in the royal ear while his flunkies
were already stretching on frames their pulled-out tongues
cleaning them of fat of impurities and tendons and handing them over
to the tanners to tan them to the shoemakers
to stretch them over their lasts . . .   *in one night*
every tenth infantryman was wearing sandals
                                                                            (the emir
before ordering his infantry on a march went to
consult the oracle—one and the same, the oracle repeats:
"in for a penny, in for a pound!")

"I order the flatterers to be brought now! let the executioner
pull out the tongue of—each of—them and . . . " said and done
fawning the voice of a boyar stepped on the august eardrum:

"since-long-long-ago-I-w-wished-to-advise-you-but-Your-wis-
dom-had-already-provided . . . "   "I also order
the orators now to be . . . "   " . . . and the stammerers"   "those
sweet-talkers the poets the sophists . . . "   " . . . and the m-m-mutes . . . ."

"I order that in place of a thousand informers
should go the hundreds of those informed on . . . "
                                                when the infantry
went out through the gate of the women's fortress
gulping down the dust stirred by the marching army there unfolded
in their throats a narrower or longer road for each but
nobody would ever be able to return on that road
                                                (the oracle
if its tongue hadn't been pulled out of its mouth oh! it
would have immediately given them the news that *the emir is dead*
not so much because troubled with doubts remorse or regrets but worn down
by his sandals made of a boyar's tongue)

6

thus spake the-Beaten-carries-the-Unbeaten:

"behold the slave how he lies prone with his spine curved
like a horseshoe (he himself doesn't believe it can bring luck!) with his ear
hearing only orders with his eyes cast down and his forehead
comfortably set under his knees like a prayer
cushion"—but what's he saying there?   "with
a mouth full (of husks) he praises his master!"—*thus
spake The-Beaten-carries-the-Unbeaten:* "behold

the head between the slave's shoulders how

it slides down his throat (don't be naïve: they aren't knots) straight
into his stomach: *here lives the brute from underground*
from here he plans rebellions new social systems
to see their aurora he stretches his skull up
from the tripe soup—how heavy it is!—as if blindfolded
seeking a way out—no there's no exit!—then lifts it
on his back under his skin like a pack of provisions like a block of salt in this way
staying hunchbacked"—but what's he shouting there?   "with
his mouth full (of husks) he curses his master!"—*thus*

spake The-Beaten-carries-the-Unbeaten:

"behold the hands of magician of class struggle
attending to his hump which went
into labor   behold in the hands of the class struggle the little hatchet
the newborn is extracted through a c-section   the method
will be generally applied during wars
on women: the bayonet the dagger and so on—the instrument differs from
case to case"—but what's he saying there?   "with
his mouth full (of husks) he names the child: Caesar!"—*thus*

spake The-Beaten-carries-the-Unbeaten:

"behold the new Caesar ordering that proofs be brought to him
("from underground!") to confirm the noble origin
of the hump   but the blood isn't blue (I fear that
through his veins flows his eternal tripe soup!)
his complexion isn't alabaster (the shape of his skull—don't ask!)
nor his chair (soft, firm) hereditary
under a torrid sun he feels the sky on top of his head like
a camel's thigh"—but what does he want there?   "with

his mouth full (of husks) he orders the slave who's carrying and jostling him
to be beaten with switches on the soles of his feet!"—*thus*

spake The-Beaten-carries-the-Unbeaten:

"behold the slave—the same one as in the first stanza—transcend-
ing his human condition he guillotines the Caesar born
out of his hump (doubtless of noble origin—
the head between his two shoulders)   behold the slave's hands
raising on a pole from the basket the head of
the dead Caesar   behold the slave's courage how he shouts with
his mouth full (of husks) in the Caesar's ear: ÉGALITÉ!

until the head of the dead Caesar swells like a balloon until
he sticks out his tongue at the slave   behold the slave's spine taking the shape
of a horseshoe: he himself doesn't believe it can bring luck!!"—*thus*
spake The-Beaten-carries-the-Unbeaten

8

"99 mouths, where are you going?"
"99 mouths, we're going along the road along the shoulder
of the road along the path along the trail
only to eat and to gobble up
99 calves of 99 barren cows
99 piglets of 99 piggybanks that feel like farrowing
99 chicks of 99 red easter eggs
99 gunnysacks of wheat from 99 swept attics
99 horseshoe nails from 99 ghosts . . . "
"99 mouths, don't go eat

99 calves of 99 barren cows, etc.

99 gunnysacks of wheat from 99 swept attics, etc.

but go eat 99 barren cows

that have eaten 99 cows with pretty faces

and plump bodies and one still can't tell

but go eat 99 swept attics

that have eaten 99 gunnysacks of wheat and one still can't tell . . . "

"99 mouths, we went along the way

along the path along the road along the shoulder

of the road towards the sunset in the Dark Foreign Lands

where smooth rupturewort doesn't grow

where the dead cow doesn't moo and the black rooster doesn't crow

we've also gone to hold-your-tongue

we mourned we wailed

that we be granted crying at least."

"99 mouths, whom do you want to cry about? . . . "

"99 mouths, we'd cry about 99 mouths

that didn't eat 99 calves of 99 barren cows

that have eaten 99 cows with pretty faces

and plump bodies and one still can't tell, etc.

that didn't eat 99 gunnysacks of wheat from 99 swept attics

that have eaten 99 gunnysacks of wheat and one still can't tell, etc."

"99 mouths, and where did the 99 mouths

look for what to eat?"

"99 mouths, those 99 mouths went . . . "

10

don quixote rising up to his belt from the machine-

for-grinding-sancho-panza   a being like the breath of

a newborn on clay feet: The-Beaten-carries-the-Unbeaten
gets half a body outside
existence—"Wó-orthy is he!"—his friday shadow
falls across the weekend: from its velvet-like fall the mourners make
capes in which they'd round him up
off the streets but the streets have stuck to his feet

he's neither here nor there—then when he appears, his presence
stirs absence everywhere around:

"I'll die: I feel how the space peels
off me   this landscape gnawed away as if by gangrene
tears itself directly off my vision   the fever is a sickness
of my skin   I can no longer feel my breath   my hands
stretch ahead of me and I run ahead to gouge out my eyes as in a game
of hide-and-seek: nothing and no one have I ever caught!   only
the refrain I know from somewhere   listen to it:

> *I've kept saying I'm going going on*
> *and no one believed me*
> *but now they'll believe me*
> *for I'll long be gone"*

                                                    his absence spreads itself

like the tablecloth at a wake   pure and white
at the beginning, stained and full of food scraps and wine spills when the housewives
shake it (shake him) to the rhythm of "Wó-orthy is he!"—*and his body*
is of everything except no longer of being

12

The-Beaten-carries-the-Unbeaten and me all three of us
stepped with our feet into an emptiness
like into a noose or a trap or—damn!—the gaping jaws
of a beast with iron teeth   I kicked my leg in the air but it didn't come off
I slammed the foot against the rocks but the emptiness didn't come off
I scraped it roughly—   gave it a scratch—   like a ball of clay—
it didn't peel off   it wouldn't detach   it didn't fall away
and since then The-Beaten-carries-the-Unbeaten and me all three of us
we wander the road (always back-and-forth like the black ribbon of a typewriter)
leaving holes in space and pauses in time   the first says:

"the drunkard and the lame man made a bet they could walk like everyone else but the lame
                                man's
still lame—he steps into emptiness and apologizes: a gra-ave! a gra-ve!   the drunkard's
still a drunkard—he gets lost walking in seven different directions and apologizes: a gra-ave!
                        a gra-ve!
the truth can't ask to be excused!"

        "God puts ideas in chains,
says the second one, you can follow the right path all your life and still
someone who's lost can step to the side and snap! . . . "

I the third one keep silent and listen—what can I
say to them? what parable? what *ars poetica*? metaphysical nothingness? while the truth is
stark naked: the manuscript of his novel being confiscated Grossman surrendered
to the KGB even the black ribbon of his typewriter

back-and-forth on a road black like the black ribbon of the typewriter
The-Beaten-carries-the-Unbeaten and me all three of us rove through the field

of metaphysics: before our eyes came   Gog and Magog
                                         Polly and Molly
                                         Haua and Bordea
they summoned us in turn denounced us estranged us
from each other turned our faces from
each other and this way set each of us against the other
without hands and feet they drove him away and caught him
without knives they sliced him up
without salt they soaked him in brine without fire they roasted him
without a mouth they ate him

                  . . . but he didn't sit well in their bellies! they felt an emptiness in the gut
how it sucks at them and joins their chest to their back   "a gra-ave! a gra-ve!"—
they screamed begged for help put two fingers down their throats—through their mouths
and nostrils I came back up with hiccups and bile before the emptiness
closed over them like the waters of the swamp seething above them
closed over them like the waters of the swamp seething above them
closed over them like the waters of the swamp seething above them

The-Beaten-carries-the-Unbeaten and me all three of us brothers
in the same shackles we drag emptiness for many years heavier than a cannonball
(that's to say: as *tramps!*)

leaving our tracks in space and spaces in time

back-and-forth on a road black like the black ribbon of the typewriter
and the flags shout ("a-uuuuuu!") at the top of their lungs with full mouths?:
                                         a gra-ave! a gra-ve!

with a shroud, on Sunday, the tailor mends the common grave in the flag
 "one at a time!" order the field jackets still unrolling the road

from our feet like film footage to deliver to the archive   while they
blindfold us with a black ribbon across our eyes (. . .)   in turn
they lead us to . . . the single file whispers into our ears: a gra-ave! a gra-ve!

"Fire!"

an eclipse, a circumcised sun

translated by
Adam J. Sorkin and Diana Manole

Ch-ău
(ragtime)

Ch-ău city on the plain plopped in the road like cow dung

                    Ch-ău city of darkness

                              city of ebonite

a madman spins it on his pinkie like a disc and a million feet

walk always hurriedly from the outskirts to the center in a circle a spiral

where emptiness yawns open in place of the Bell Tower

                         along-
side the city's first pay toilets
you buy a ticket and sitting in the stall you try your luck but—you bet wrong!
1 9 (these are your first numbers) make ten and (the other two)
7 1 make eight—the year you first saw asphalt pavement and houses with nine
or even more storeys   only a hundred steps away from the stalls
God snatched you then *from under a car's wheels*
dressed in blue jeans to go to school for a few days
you grow up make your parents happy go away return

                         capital city
with a name like you've turned on the water tap while you . . . Ch-(ish)-
in-a white sink where the prime ministers wash their hands
replaced in just a year (ah this whiteness only the sleeve
of the black compact-disc *the Ch-ău*)

                    spinning in its nothingness

suddenly revealing its gauzy lingerie like Lautrec's
Dancers with "have you seen what we can do?"

                                           asleep on their feet
Christ and Judas swing around till they change places once more
half past one on the grandfather clock whose hands they themselves are

                                                          the ventriloquist
sits next to the president (barely understanding Romanian he
flaps his lips while the ventriloquist speaks
about the C.I.S. and the Independence of Republics)

Ch-ău city like a hand clapped across a mouth   providence
fails to descend upon a group of comrades on an ordinary
business trip

                                 obtaining a tourist visa
makes you as happy as obtaining MFN status

you imagine yourself as Guan Yin waiting for *Lao-Tzu*
to dedicate to you The Tao
of Power before he takes leave through the western gate

you see the mothers of champions nursing their offspring with Cola-Cao

you've reached out an open hand to the belly begging for spare change

you have a body cursed to share between Annas
and Caiaphas you have the right to vote *The Freedom to Shoot a Gun*
a woman locked into her body like a panther in a cage
The Central Cemetery on Armenească Street a good place for eternal rest and a walk
you have something she lacks

and the exact measure of her demands
you have the city that the madman spins on his pinkie at 33 rpm
even if you stood still you'd be like a needle in the groove

Ch-ău black halo like the driven nail with an onyx gleam

casting a spell: "dry sun from first light
                         from midday from afternoon
                         from the setting of the sun
                         from the middle of the night
                         from the roosters' crowing
                         from daybreak's light growing
                         dry sun with the incarnation
                         dry sun with incantation
                         dry sun with the knife
                         dry sun with the stake
                         sun dry white black . . . "

                                              you have the national boor
who made it in through the Senate's door
you're appalled by anthologies your liver has great pain
you'll give up the ghost but I don't give a damn
                              since others are gone who had more to live for

the symbol with Jesus's age on the LP
tells it the appropriate speed

they saw you waltz with Sadness a fat broad
(every other man in the city has had her)
you open your eyes where two highways have their start
and you passionately follow the two-way traffic

you see (since childhood until the putsch when they took it down)
Lenin's monument barbaric symbolic phallic you see the Triumphal
Arch like a swinging gate which he tries to
S-O S(!)educe—so you see Ten Thousand Creatures
ADAM-ites and EVA-cuees through car doors casinos prison bars
you see the Corn Cob thick as a bunker flattened like the forehead
of an agronomist where the members of parliament often start
a mămăligă the headquarters of the Central Committee (an ex) shaped like a crampon
The Cathedral fallen to its knees like an old hag
kissing the cross of the metropolitan (ours?) of Ch-ău Vladimir
dark as in an asshole

                              you notice the typo on the front page of the newspaper
the president Mircea Snegur becomes Sne*cur* a sneaky ass

you close your eyes you direct traffic—it's easy—
through the tunnels (two) carved in the bones   you listen to Pergolesi
Stabat Mater

                    a gigantic disc-city its ecstatic spinning transmitting the sound
                    (posthumously)
of singers Ion Aldea and Doina   on their fatal last ride
Ten Thousand came out to accompany them as an honor guard along the flanks of their
                              passage
like a train borne by the page Void and the chambermaid Et Cetera

Ch- (rist may have in His name) ău

wasteland where nothing is
                              ragtime
                                        the abyss

the void expanding dead-center in the disc ready to overflow the edge
of the record   a hole thanks to which it spins
faster and faster: 33 - 45 - 78—a windmill

click click click

in the end you turn the page
                    (the hand
                                the cheek
                                    the tickets
                                            the back)

you turn the record   the same ending: *and in emptiness and in plenitude the value hides*
the value hides   hides the value   value

translated by
Adam J. Sorkin and Diana Manole

The Fan

1. "By His will Eve in the mystery of Genesis open to my hands like a fan"—

2.

the evangelist writes through revelation. I have only one real woman (ah, her name
doesn't appear transparent like filigree in any
syllable of my name to give it the least
value) and her flesh if joyous her books unread or not I shall write
"by His will Eve in the mystery of Genesis open to my hands like a fan
(. . . folded from the aurora borealis light of the body
on the first night of love)." I have only one real woman—raw material
for an initiation into making poetry: her dainty geisha hand I press tightly
counting phalanges, lines from a tanka and a haiku
are in her pinkie and in the empty space
between her fingers shimmers transparently the-poem-to-
be-read-between-the-lines. on her naked body clings the flowered kimono
of the silk of syntax, through the sleeves allowing
a glimpse of the coy flesh of the caterpillar in a cocoon.
I have only the fair soft caterpillar which I open and squeeze as it makes sounds as if
with an accordion with firm breasts *stammering with happiness*. pleats & cones
of darkness. in the dance rhythm of Maria Tănase's "The Mulberry Orchard" there's only
a screen of gestures from the shadow play. only the shadows
on the eyelids, in their fluttering like a butterfly wing
shaking their pollen until transparency. a membrane
gathered of space. hymen of
the Blessed Mother. and again" I have only one real woman . . . only
her dainty geisha hand . . . only the tanka and haiku and empty space
between her fingers from where there appears the-poem-to-
be-read-between-the-lines:

in His solitude, God
tends the garden
hates prying eyes.
so as not to upset him, I cover
my face with the fan.

3.

a) then on the wedding night into her body of supreme joy descends
transcendence. "I'm sorry for the trouble," she says, "I'll sleep until tomorrow
morning in the marriage bed of the body of supreme joy (it suffices how much
I've kept trembling all night in martyrs and saints' bodies and living holy relics
—biers of bones and benches made of *demi-vierges* and stale air!—
let others also sleep wherever it steals over them . . .)
I stretch myself only as long as it won't bother either of them at dawn I
sip a short coffee smoke a cigar listen to the hymn check my watch
upon the third crowing of the cock take my doll and go away

leaving you in *the human condition* . . . "

. . . and the next day, at the crack of dawn, without looking back
over her shoulder ay! without regret from her body of supreme joy she'd exit
on tiptoe—the step of a one-night wife ("*show me yourself
naked . . .*" the refrain echoes in his ears still —the beauty
without a body ("*How beautiful she is . . .*") leaving—for whom?—

b) the bed sheets—every which way—like a blank form. I see my body
extended from left to right like handwriting
filling in the form. with bulging eyes as if circumcised I stare at
the-one-who-doesn't-have-a-body-entering-into-the-one-who-doesn't-have-flaws
how she gently pulls me towards the shore
to drown me in the eternal sleep. how stretching my body to the side

I was pulled to, she circumscribes me as if in a state
of siege (the white flags of the flesh at half-staff): it's
three o'clock in the morning, forever, day after day. I see my body
laid down . . . the-one-who-doesn't-have-flesh-entering-into-the-one-who-doesn't-have-flaws
asking me: *"should we*
let it wrinkle? . . . "

4.

"my hands, dear sisters, what did you do when the Father, in anger,
banished me from heaven on the lost path through brambles on a road of no return
utterly naked and henceforth banished?"

"I kept turning everywhere: on the eyes neck cheeks indiscreet fullness on
the thighs and the breasts a fan with a membrane of air and spokes of bone
a grape leaf hiding the nakedness henceforth banished."

"I kept turning everywhere: plucking from the thighs clusters of
frightened hands, plucking from the sex and eyes clusters of
gestures twisted like spiders weaving a shroud on the nakedness
of the body of supreme joy.

she reached out two hands, different as two Marys: Blessed Mother and whore.

but, opening them, the palms of both hands, so that I'd kiss her between
her fingers (at the joint, there from where they start shy like snail
antennae), one by one, ay! between each pair of fingers revealed to me
a *vagina dentata*. there, from where . . .
she reached out two hands different as two Marys: 'guess which one I'm in?'

I laughed, didn't say anything . . . "—
                                        writes

the evangelist, with his left hand writing over what he's just written with his right

(see ch. 6)

5.

endless like space, as if it dressed in maya's *haute couture*, when she unfolds
among the first born of each branch of Adam's descent,
each of the first born being a rib
of the fan of her endless body

who goes from hand to hand asking coquettishly: "who doesn't have in his grasp the gentle
    north breeze?"

who now divides herself into time zones and for me alone hasn't even *one hour and then
    must die*

who carries on her back a veil of glances who trails behind her a train of eyes like a
    peacock *whoever sees her / can never forget her*

who removes her garments (while you try to guess from a daisy's petals: "she loves me?" or
    "she loves me not? . . . ")

who leads her lovers through embraces polished like the blades of a meat grinder ("only
    our flesh still knows her perfume")

who loses her lovers at Russian roulette, "та-та, та-та-та-та, та-та, а точнее сказать я не
    вправе"*

---

* (Russian) "ta-ta, ta-ta-ta-ta, ta-ta, / and more exactly i'm not allowed to say"—lines from the poem
"Slava" ("Glory") by Vladimir Nabokov.

who makes a hot day cool a shadow on a long afternoon
from the closed eyes from the still nostrils from the
corners of the lips the flies

who arcs between God and you like a rainbow, opening
into bands of samsara light

to whom *today the One above Existence gives life*

who comes as if she'd leave forever who *still*
gathers strength for another step / for she arrived and enchained me

who trembles in creases so that she fills her mirror with wrinkles (the same
      little mirror with only one answer: " . . . fairest of them all!") when
      the betrothal-time comes, dressed up, to lift
      the skirt, her flesh like marilyn's little white dress

who *who'd'ya give it to, bitch?* . . .

6.

"unrewarded and naked she's bound to the pillar on which she tied me naked and
        unrewarded.
face to face like day and night I embraced the pillar
and the black monk, boredom, kept whipping / flaying us with
God's pulled-out tongue, braided from the six commandments of Nativity,
until we unbound ourselves, struggling. until the first commandment was broken.
. . . and it was evening and it was morning: lovers and bosom friends
thus the *first* day found us

unbegun, her wave bound to the pillar to which I'm tied with the wave, myself unbegun.

face to face like waters from waters yet unparted I embraced the pillar
and the purple monk, tedium, kept whipping / flaying us with
God's pulled-out tongue, braided from the six commandments of Nativity,
until we unbound ourselves, struggling. until the second commandment was broken.
 . . . and it was evening and it was morning: lovers and bosom friends
thus the *second* day found us

unstained, her shadow bound to the pillar to which I'm tied with the shadow, myself
        unstained.
face to face like the shore and the waters I embraced the pillar
and the yellow monk, trouble, kept whipping / flaying us with
God's pulled-out tongue, braided from the six commandments of Nativity,
until we unbound ourselves, struggling. until the third commandment was broken.
 . . . and it was evening and it was morning: lovers and bosom friends
thus the *third* day found us

unparalleled, by her blood bound to the pillar to which I'm tied by blood, myself unparalleled.
face to face like the moon and the sun I embraced the pillar
and the dark red monk, longing, kept whipping / flaying us with
God's pulled-out tongue, braided from the six commandments of Nativity,
until we unbound ourselves, struggling. until the fourth commandment was broken.
 . . . and it was evening and it was morning: lovers and bosom friends
thus the *fourth* day found us

unbodied, by its speech bound to the pillar to which I'm tied by speech, myself unbodied.
face to face like the born and the unborn I tightly embraced the pole
and the gray monk, blame, kept whipping / flaying us with
God's pulled-out tongue, braided from the six commandments of Nativity,
until we unbound ourselves, struggling. until the fifth commandment was broken.
 . . . and it was evening and it was morning: lovers and bosom friends
thus the *fifth* day found us

unworldly, by sorcery bound to the pillar to which I'm tied by sorcery, myself unworldly.
face to face like man and woman I embraced the pillar
and the feeble monk, with three faces, doesn't hear doesn't see doesn't understand, kept
                                        whipping / flaying us with
God's pulled-out tongue, braided from the six commandments of Nativity,
until we unbound ourselves, struggling. until the sixth commandment was broken.
. . . and it was evening and it was morning: lovers and bosom friends
thus the *sixth* day found us—
                        the evangelist writes
on the *seventh* day between the folds of the fan, the

7.

fan that shuts tight into a bone handle, bone out of which once upon a time *Eve fan-atic* . . .

translated by
Adam J. Sorkin and Diana Manole

" $V_A{}^{cc}{}_A\sim$ "

our father who art in heaven you are the iron stake as I on earth am
       the cow tethered to you by the rope *moo*[1]

2.

which rope is a predicate because: 1) it shows what the subject is doing and 2) it answers
the question *what's going on*? the family school taught me
that the subject is "cow": it pulls out—
the active voice—the stake. as a child they *cow*ed me by *vacc*inating me anti-
god: for me they pulled out the stake
my earthly father the puppeteer brought it to the junkyard he took me by the rope
and led me to school like an ox on a lead to learn
together with other milksops and mooncalves to ask
the question I knew the answer to. I was on the point of
coming back like a cow. oh innocence lost together with the first "why is it?"
and as to a child who surprised his parents
making love, so truth showed itself to me. I recognized it: I must *moo*-
ve on to the next world! it was as if I'd been born again: I tugged on
my bedsheets though I remained motionless. only the rope *moo*
vibrated and its vibration filled the air with
circumvolutions. "there's no light
anywhere . . . " since then I've had dark circles under my eyes. always ready
to tie myself to the rope *moo*—the reflexive
voice—around my neck. for a long time since then it's been only knots. as I tried to
get to its point it passed through my hands
like a string of rosary beads: a lot of the time merely "why is it?" and again the same "why?"
until the words perhaps are melted together—the passive voice—
by the rope *moo* I will be led to him. like he who stays and wants to
swallow the moon as in that poem in verses

Tibi vero gratias agam quo clamore? Amore more ore re^2
I swallow a letter until it sticks in my throat *ore re-*

3.

ality: with four legs an udder horns a tail on the tip of which
quotation marks make a whiskbroom. oh, when I was a wee lad following along at the
        cow's tail
never was I sent to tend the cow—my relation with
the quadruped being established by this association: as a little kid
when I played a prank my grandmother yelled at me
"you pharaoh!" my flesh—seven white cows fat with milk eaten up by seven black and ill
favored cows—since then
it's a frightful nightmare from which I wake up—to interpret
it—and send for the priest. and the priest sends for
the bell ringer. and he sends for the gravedigger. at the command "one two three up!" they
        pick
the slave right out of his prison cell (it goes without saying
they didn't have a clue about what anton pavlovich said: "everyday
you have to squeeze the slave out of you") and they hurriedly present him to me. his words
strike my ears as through a stethoscope:

4.

"a poem is—exactly the same as an empire. what is
an empire? exactly the same as the stomach of a bovine—sing
along with us *the cow grazes*
the grass so green . . . —with two larders: the bigger one is like a storehouse
where grass lies down in its green nightshirt and night
wakes up in coarse striped twill in the little
larder, which in fact sustains digestion. ('don't

be sad,' father said, 'you're leaving

a larger prison for a narrower one') I built

a fifth of the country—sing

along with us *the flowers*

flourish in the fields . . . —and I locked it up in the little larder. we put

guards all around. we put on a dog collar of

electricity and I threw the muzzle away. I sicced it on and

set it loose at the barbed wire and (' . . . but

you won't be happy when you get out,' he went on saying, 'you'll just change

a narrower prison for a larger one') in this way

we handed out handouts and we had the upper hand. repeat

along with us: a poem

is—exactly the same as an empire. it has the stomach

of a bovine: hardly has it swallowed words when it starts

to digest them: its milk

we ourselves *drink it in the evening we drink it at noon in the morning we drink it and at*

night we drink it

and we drink it.[3] signed: iosif vis-

5.

sarionovich and his brothers." an expansive poetry an endless poetry just like

latitude 66° 33' north the poem goes round and round.

we have been deported beyond the arctic circle of thought we subjects with warm

blood in our hearts where transcendence descends from the sky along thousands

of rope *moos* in the likeness of snow and hangs

like a marionette in the heavens where space

makes one with time: wildly stripping off the aurora

borealis as if a *shirt for which they did cast lots.*[4] from this

no escape exists. only writing an expansive poetry an endless poetry just like

latitude 66° 33' north you

let yourself be convinced by the words to run away with them. *a "cow"—a poem.*[5]

6.

        "to recite
poems in prison," ion mureșan points out, "is the equivalent of organizing
a mass escape." we celebrate, mureșan cristofor and yours truly—we three kings of
orient—on the eminescu anniversary at gherla, in one end
of the huge prison "in the shape of a broad U"[6]—there's no need for us
to wave our hands above us and thus pay homage: "eminesc-U-U-U!" like at a rally—in
        one
of the cells suddenly transformed to "the big house"—quotations
from eminescu decorate the walls (a heap of towels open
and close each quotation like quotation marks) beside a map
of greater romania and "excerpts from the statutes of internment" together
with a thousand young people in coarse striped twill—oh their short
bristly hair like an english greensward cut to zero for at least ten
generations in a row—only eyes and ears, through the desire for elusive freedom—
libi. I inhale gherla air deep into my chest—not even the thickness
of my diaphragm between present and past—and I exhale the carbon dioxide of the gulag:
"osip mandelstam # the story is told # in those months
of detention # disgusted by dirt and misery # never ate
mess-hall grub # he was an unusually delicate poet # with an innate sense of
hygiene # a pure skeleton # flinging over his left shoulder
the toga of flesh # publius ovidius naso of the gulag # to
sustain his breath # he'd recite
to the common criminals # whole kilometers of poems # whereupon
they rewarded him # better than in borges's prose # royally # with a portion
of white bread every day." oh poetry, *panem et circenses.*

7.

"a very docile population. the common people. a nation with fear of
god." as if we all were born to one mother. as if
the mother gave birth to us one night in which
the black cow calved a heifer and the newly-calved heifer calved a heifer and
that heifer calved a heifer[7] from which—turned away from the tit—we sucked.

translated by
Adam J. Sorkin and Cristina Cîrstea Danilov

Notes and comments (or seven lean cows)

1. According to Tibetan religions, the first kings on earth "all had on the top of their heads a *mu* rope of light" (. . .) When they died, they dissolved (like the rainbow, beginning with their feet, and melted into the *mu* cord on the top of their heads. In turn, the *mu* rope melted in the Sky" (R.A. Stein, *La civilisation tibétaine*, pp. 189–190); also in the Quran (III, 98) we read: "Cling firmly to God's rope and do not become separated."
2. A verse by the monk Athanasius Kircher (1601–1680); literal translation: "How can I proclaim my gratitude? By your love, by your nature, by your prayers and by your deeds."
3. Line from the poem "Todesfuge" by Paul Celan (1920–1970), translated into Romanian by Petre Solomon, *Contemporanul*, 2 may 1947.
4. See the Gospel of John 19: 23–24 [in King James version]: Then the soldiers, when they had crucified Jesus, took his garments, and made four parts, to every soldier a part; and also *his* coat: now the coat was without seam, woven from the top throughout . . . They said therefore among themselves, Let us not rend it, but cast lots for it, whose it shall be: that the scripture might be fulfilled . . .
5. Paraphrase after a line by Alexandru Muşina: "A cow, a poem". In GULAG language, "cow" means prisoner taken "meat" by the group escaping from the camp. See Ryszard Kapuściński, Imperium: "When all common prisoners fled, they persuaded one of the political prisoners—who were naive and disoriented—to come with them. In this way they protected themselves against death by starvation. At a certain moment they killed their victim and shared their prey."
6. See Paul Goma, *Gherla*, Humanitas, 1990, p. 69; in the same book: "prison poetry must not be judged from the outside, not even by prisoners once they've been freed. Prison poetry has nothing in common with freedom, as freedom rejects it" (pp. 172–173).
7. See "The Burdens of Loss" in Ovidiu Bîrlea, *The Little Encyclopedia of Romanian Stories*, The Scientific and Encyclopedic Publishing House, 1976.

Iov & Vio

"He who was living is now dead
We who were living are now dying
With a little patience"
T. S. Eliot, *The Waste Land*

1.

like champagne kept in a warm place—as if 103° isn't actually a high fever!—, this body
foams with red
spots, from head to toe: "happy new year!" (saying that, you feel your tongue blistered in
your mouth,
and your speech, where before it was smooth, now covered in sores), when at the eleventh
hour not the president but the last man ("I only am escaped to tell
thee"), rather than wishing you a new beginning, gives you tidings of the end: "next year
and . . ."
(tomorrow's almost today!) exactly new year's eve. oh my aching head!
(a cork your strength twists around itself like a corkscrew, to rip it off your shoulders,
or jams inside with a spoon handle and just as much pain.)
on the morning of the first he awakens in the nightshirt of december 31
and when he tries to take it off, he's given a hospital gown instead (what can be seen *where
the garment gapes*[1] doesn't entice the eye). "sign here (with a check mark) that you've
refused
hospitalization" *V* iov.[2] "and you, that he'll be released into your custody"—vio *V*

2.

to get a head start on the gravediggers along a shortcut, not the corpse to the grave, but I'd
bear the grave to the body—and rid myself of it!
(it's a forty-plus-year-old grave for a six-foot man, his parents still alive, the head

of his family and a loving husband in his own right—neither any man's life can fill it but
now you've got to mouth off

right back to it, a grave *à fleur de tête* that would fit your foot like cinderella's slipper,

if you'd only try it on—nor any man's death find enough room in it but now you need to try
its maw.)

effing bitch! it doesn't want to slide easily down the gullet and [*Requiescat in*] *pace*! So then
I divide it, the grave, into smaller graves

like the pills in an empty blister-pack—I take them morning, noon and night but it's never-
ending.

how might you sift it through a strainer, the common grave, to find those who were yours.
How might you screen the little graves

through the silk sieve, may it turn to dust and ashes

because it's too full, the grave spills over—I've put in it all the clay I'm made of.

now a woman with a funnel (a kind of hourglass but irreversible—not the character but
her object), by

the way it drags me down, and in my final hours I'll raise it up to my mouth like a
megaphone: "*de profundis clamavi!*"

(detonating with your prior dead laid in the earth—beware! you can't begin to imagine
how the shock wave will scatter you.)

welcoming as only death can be. if only it wouldn't sit itself down on my body as on a nest
to brood over the little graves,

if it wouldn't caw so much, scratch for earthworms, take dust baths!

like a winnow with grain—this body, turned out into the dust together with the chaff, for
the young wives

to sort the good seeds from the barren. earthworm-sifter, that mothers may [. . .] the grain
for flour from the grain for funeral sweets

3.

could the body be so fragile that it must be wrapped up as in a sheet of bubble wrap
before it's mailed—*poste restante*—from this world to the next?

and the recipient whose name's written on the parcel, when he finally receives it, could he

be so blind that he'll have need of the blisters' braille to

read in its soul? and the soul,

so fragile that it must be worn under a covering of skin and bones sprinkled with soft

pearls

that will ripen and hatch? or will he, precisely as in Dante's *Inferno*, arrive *de son vivant*

in the cast-iron cauldrons of tar and when he reaches the boiling point blow—S.O.S.—air

bubbles?

if the spirit goes to heaven and spirits go to the head, —a pox on that!—why does the body

turn topsy-turvy

like a strong țuică that swirls and makes bubbles?

the answer: "let us live—

to remember"

4.

to each disease there should correspond, if not a band that plays at weddings and funerals,

then one musical instrument.

a different one, that is, from person to person. god—you've just discovered—doesn't beat

you with a stick, he quietly taps on your body

as on his stand with a baton (exactly like, in the silence between the movements, fear of

death: "and what if there's no conductor

at his desk?") iov's quartet was a trio: *iov & vio.* listen for yourself

how affliction transforms the bodily organs into instruments of grief without removing

them from their sheaths of skin, with closed eyes.

even you can see that, struck by grace, the flesh gets dotted with sores like a musical score

with notes. you realize

that finally, touched to the marrow of your bones, this ever hollower body becomes one

with the magic

flute when it laments: *"o remember that my life is a breath of wind!"*

you took forty-plus years to master it; from your workshops arose

strings, keyboards, brass, percussion, woodwinds *et cetera* (and the proud man!), as many
as needed to fill the pit
of an orchestra-la-la / to escort an entire village to the grave in this rhythm: *do do doo-be*
doo-be do-ay!

until it returns for you, now in third-person singular: *doo-be doo-be away! / he's lived his day*

5.

can you be vaccinated against the brass? against the cymbals?—when they call you by name
as *sounding*
brass / clanging cymbal. after which, year after year, you have fed from the palm of your hand
the singing bird that alights in a row, like a flock of swallows along telegraph wires, from the
keys to the chords,
can you divine your future—while you know neither your past nor . . . —in its entrails?
does the holy spirit, who takes shelter in wood, fear maggots the same way other breathing
things fear worms?
with eight holes and passed through fire, the ocarina is a miniature replica of the body sitting
among the ashes—is it
bringing fire upon itself, said to be the end? have you heard what the potsherd says to the
broken pot when they meet?
the answer: *"curse God and die!"*

6.

wriggling in my skin as on hospital bed sheets unchanged on schedule—because they expected
the patient would give up the ghost—so that upon awakening I can't remember my own
features, as if you'd transcribed by hand
in the latin alphabet a text printed in cyrillic: *kak mne huiovo!*[3] and instead of praising the lord
day and night, my tongue outdoes itself with filth: "go fuck the day I was
born!", "*ieba io ti mrtvu matku pod levim sisom na hladnom grobe!*"[4]—an aristo-croat lady

among a gang of lowlifes—"suck night's cock when it was said: *there is*
a man child conceived!"
(inscribe in the flesh, the mistake to have been *made* from birth is the letter of the law;
there's no more eagle-eyed proofreader on the face of the earth than death! 5 liters of
blood, ever renewed—
to last a lifetime!—are at your disposal for you to make the correction: *"I'll be as if I've*
never been!"
and then—for 24 years now, yet still the same—vio comes, with her blood refreshed month
after month, and writes to me
life *с красной строки*[5]
(see *kali*graphic poem)

7.

as if you planted a hundred-pound sack of potatoes in holes and behind you molehills kept
mounding up—such blindness!
on the earth, I looked like a garden plot after a meteor shower, before it changed its name,
from
the potter's—the blood garden, as I keep scraping myself with a shard of clay. under my skin
there moves about
a still-young grave, filled up to here with picture postcards of the other world, which I raise
like a pedigreed boar,
waiting for resurrection from the dead. (and the same thought always scraping inside my
brain like a butcher's
knife: if life's merely a mire of pigshit, much better had it not been given to the boar; life
eternal, give that
to us today, like a piggybank as fat as a sow—for us to smash again and again, day and night!
now I know: "the wisdom of the earth" giving herself in love to a man gone crazy with
sores on his sore head is the most eloquent proof that, among all things, not the most beautiful,
but the only impossible one is the best choice, just as *the year in which you die is your good*
year.[6]

not quite an itching of the tongue but rather a tingling of desire, my words parch

the roof of my mouth, to the same extent as your lips turn moist (I'll be discreet and keep
private which lips),

and I didn't say everything yet, I didn't say anything.

or: how would you dig up a treasure so its flames pass into you—in the form of a burn? an
illumination?

in a country (mini) like a suffix, a diminutive, I lived forty-plus years . . . like a footnote

in small print, without knowing how many lines of text separate me from the word which

I make reference to—the thought of this kept me going all these years; one time only

he remembered me but then he lost me on a simple bet!

as long as one man's life (1879–1953), that country (1917–1991)[7] composed through a
perpetual suffixation—set its candle among *the dead*;

on its account, charge it with more than 60,000,000 human lives lost. *no man's land.*

whoever makes babies in such a country at the same time digs them—*locus pessimus atque
profundus*—their grave.

now I see: "the wisdom of the earth" takes as her husband a man too dumb to come out of
the rain making the ideal

couple, hence life expectancy proves favorable to women, *'cause love's like death.*

about the way words couple, ask what the first hundred—men and women—who were
hotshots

at tree felling in the gulag, and allowed in the same barracks overnight together—promised
to each other.

and I didn't say everything yet, I didn't say anything.

maybe neither one thing nor another: as if you transplanted a cemetery, trees and all, and
only the crosses took root (*INRI*)—a poor excuse for a
resurrection!

thank god, I wasn't subservient or *innocent*—on the lawn of books grazes "$V_A CC_A\sim$"; in
diverse languages; my own child,

quite alive, and to me, too, childhood returned, at an age when *disease doesn't air the rooms,*
like chickenpox[8]

(as if the weather were howling out of *Ecclesiastes*: "the wind goes towards the south and
turns about . . . "). owing one death,

I don't run away from my eternal creditor at the world's end—*lest sarmatian soil should
cover my bones!* —, I don't hold a symposium on

my sickbed. rather I ask myself: what if, instead of saying what they thought, as witnesses
for the prosecution, although they believed

themselves on the side of the defense, the three of them—eliphaz the temanite, and bildad
the shuhite, and zophar the naamathite —

had been more openhanded and paid for job's treatment, the way mircea nedelciu's friends,

with money they raised at an auction at the literature museum, kept him alive for five more
years?

(as if, plighted to perdition, life gets ransomed in small change. though

my hide—put through the mill until it has turned into a strainer for worms—isn't even
worth tanning.)

epidermal, my complete poetry is in vio's hands—on her lifeline.

I said everything. I didn't say anything.

Ch-ău, 9 mai–5 august, 2010

*translated by
Adam J. Sorkin and Diana Manole*

1. Quotation from Roland Barthes, *The Pleasure of the Text*: "Is not the most erotic portion of a body *where the garment gapes?*"
2. The name Job in Romanian is *iov*.
3. (Russian; vulgar) I'm in deep shit!
4. (Croatian; vulgar) Fuck your dead mother under her left tit on the cold casket!
5. (Russian) literally: outside the red line, i.e., outside the paragraph.
6. Quotation from Aurel Dumitraşcu, *The Good Year*.
7. Stalin, Iosif Vissarionovici (1879–1953); USSR (1917–1991).
8. Paraphrase after Dan Coman: "I'm 27. I'm in my own house. disease airs the rooms" (*poem at 27*).

Afterword: *Sang d'encre*

A reed with the head of romantic Christ impaled on top: this is Emilian Galaicu-Păun on the street. But neither the reed nor the Christ image, joined in a casual sacredness, remains a strictly ordinary, city-sidewalk emblem. On the contrary, they participate deeply in poetry, not only in its thematic structure but also in the dialectics and subterranean vision. On the primary level, the real and the corporeal (with the latter raised to a privileged position, as a victim of textual vampirism) are explored in a symbolic mode, while sacredness is consecrated by a realistic method (with a hint of sarcastic annoyance when it reaches complete alienation). On the secondary level, they merge into a physical writing of enlightenment, or an enlightened literature of sensations. Indeed, the two kinds of writing interweave in turn, until they are indistinct in a kind of fabric at once tight and loose, in which impulsiveness is restrained by meticulousness and the summons of gravity by a consciousness of artifact and play.

As an existential undertaking, equally programmatic and structural, Galaicu-Păun's poetry is a maximalist one, driven to reveal the epiphany of death and to illuminate the meanings in the silence of the words' grave, not without undergoing frivolous adventures, in which the poet consciously involves himself and which he experiences as ludic ecstasy. It is then a hermeneutic poetics, engaged in the elucidation of the meanings hidden in words—not in words indifferent to the real, such as those proposed by Hermogenes, but rather in ones that properly contain the real, according to Cratylus's claims. A poetics, therefore, still asserting the ontological, the last romantic vestige in postmodern culture, which Galaicu-Păun openly, if not even ostentatiously, professes, not only through intertextual doping but also through a domesticated post-avant-gardism that also nonetheless relishes experimental adventure, using text as a playground and—likewise—as the site for formal experiments.

Even the emblem under which he gathers his poems—that of *Canting Arms*—preserves the sense of action, relying on the syntagm's ambiguity as symbolic sublimation and enciphering of the real, alongside its heraldic meaning: poetry is participation, not just gratuitous play and, implicitly, the denial of ontological responsibility. On the contrary, it is a powerful, redemptive language meant at least to censor the fatality of death, the one who "seeks" the poet "by the midwife." This is the radiant core—indeed impossible to exorcise—of Galaicu-Păun's poetry: the overlapping of birth and death, their inseparability, their oneness. It is a core of imperative anxiety that poetry cannot unravel, since it is only its expression, not its remedy: "poetry is like death on the bridal bed and birth on the deathbed." Poetry is likewise hymn and lament: lament when it praises and hymn when it mourns. It is an oxymoronic equation in which contraries not only merge, but each takes the place of the other.

This nucleus then reverberates at all levels of his poems, transforming the texts into a contorted means to balance and harmonize opposites: creative vertigo on one hand and the technique of managing fulminant outbursts thorough craftmanship on the other. Galaicu-Păun relies on the unleashed natural violence of the imaginary, discharged through rich expressionist tensions in which the revelation has the concrete immediacy of a spasm, and the spasm has the diaphanous—and also unbearable—grammar of a mystery. Thus derives a poetry of high-voltage seizures—or earthquakes—of both the being and the language, a poetry as if barely escaped from the terror of vision, one that reflects on the page the vaguely controlled panic of its imaginative furor. From a furor grounded in Romanticism, the poetry of Galaicu-Păun draws its visionary principle and even its reports of everyday detail. For him, the brutal insertions of the real and burning sarcasm express a state of prophetic fever; they are not simply transcriptions but violent insertions of anxiety, and the real, no matter how immediate, is actually projected not as a notation but as imaginative hypothesis and state, as entropic epiphanies.

Galaicu-Păun's poetry is a volcanic, baroque discourse, expansive in its themes and relentless in its imaginative avalanches (and no less in its referential play), aiming to accumulate in itself all the valences of an emotional state, condition, or symbol, which for him always form an inextricable knot, on the criterion of visionary exhaustiveness (of a hermeneutic vision).

At least in appearance, his work sets in contrast the principles of visionary expansiveness and the writer's tendency to expand with depth and essentialization. And, of course, there would be no contradiction if they were not employed at the same time, in the attempt to reconcile two poetics that seem to exclude each other categorically. However, Galaicu-Păun's poetry essentializes even as it gets loose, and it also stretches at the very moment when the vision dramatically contracts. Not in turn, not in alternation, but with one and the same move, it thus vexes the baroque through short streaks of lightning and justifies its concentration through discursive explosions in a chain reaction.

The principle of this impossible synthesis is a kind of a structural oxymoron of his vision, willing to dwell exclusively in opposites that reveal each other. The same principle of impossible synthesis also operates at the level of his constructive abilities, applied in such a way as to create a drastic contrast between the visionary electricity of some sequences and the detailed craftsmanship (including intertextual games, subtle deconstructions, and erudite arrangements) of others, between impetuosity and diligence. The uncontrollable explosions seem held back by a shrewdness at creating subtleties, and the fevered vision seems to cool under the effect of masterful literary passages. There are, of course, two rhythms of his poetic vision, two speeds, one precipitous, the other measured; but here, too, it is not about alternative speeds or rhythms, but simultaneous actions that provoke one another; or, at the very least, the slow pace of meticulousness is only the means of setting in motion the eruptive rhythm.

However, Galaicu-Păun usually proceeds at both speeds at the same time. No wonder he requires long, wide textual highways and extensive textual orchestration, and not just of the poems themselves, but of entire volumes. No doubt it is precisely the electricity of the ultimate anguish at the core of his poetics that requires a manifest repetitiveness (let alone a circularity) of themes, but it is no less true that a premeditated symphonic structure is intended. There are motifs that unite (actually merge) the poems, there are symbols that appear throughout most of the poems, there are lines that echo from poem to poem. This does not account for the equally contorted and pedantic syntax also meant to ritualize the text and to ensure for the imagination's brutal levitation an opportunity for textual slowing, for liturgical recital.

The fundamental contradiction between the sacred and the baroque, between the decantation of essences and the invention of details, resolves itself through a sort of diachronic vampirism. Although it seems extensive and expansive, Galaicu-Păun's principle of writing is extremely restrictive. His books swallow one another, each of them absorbing the essence of the preceding ones, not necessarily repeating texts but taking up anew, in other visionary dimensions, the identical network of symbols and the identical issues of the human condition. Only the inability to write directly the ultimate book, the book of essences or "the Book of Books," persuaded Galaicu-Păun to approach it through successive approximations. For, otherwise, his vision constitutes a pyramidal project, and the expansiveness of writing is nothing other than the perverse effect of the contracting vision and of the implosive concentration of significances.

The imagination's spontaneous impulse to unleash nature's violence is contrasted—and relativized—on the one hand by a stylistics of details processed in symbolic terms and on the other hand by an intertextual imagination going beyond a tenacious memory that breaks forth constantly in quotes and references. Since his is the kind of poetry that has not settled into being purposeless, Galaicu-Păun turns ink into blood—and blood into ink, of course (see "*sang d'encre*"). At a confessional level, his work is a biographical vampire (but not an exhibitionist) that feeds on the biography of the poet himself, with enough sequences recorded live and with raw reality, sometimes even excessive in its immediacy, but promising the poet a certain fervor in the symbolic rendering of domestic gestures. On the principle of raising each and every gesture and detail to a symbol, sensual or even sexual euphoria is thus transformed into symbolic orgies, into allegorical or just anagogical tournaments. Galaicu-Păun in fact favors a symbolic reading of the real, even where concrete notations are piled up in grotesque heaps (in the long poems of moral and existential despair, of vituperative anger and denunciation).

But his "real," no matter how rich, is always already cultured, already formalized, already a signifier. It partakes immediately of an allegorizing process and an organizing scheme, a symbolic structure. And as this process cannot be stopped, as reality has an irrepressible impulse to turn into symbols, the poem must transcribe the braiding, the overlaps, the fusion; it becomes the point of convergence of as many disparate elements as possible, coalescing from biography, memory, everyday life, imagination, the library, the poet's skill. The effervescence of these sudden occurrences puts the poet in the position of giving them symbolic ductility, setting them in one direction and harmonizing their potential for meaning.

A cumulative, multifaceted literature is born, the purpose of which is to blend in a unity of sense the strident, centrifugal registers:

> when I'm about to turn the corner, it should happen the same way that in the
> > scaffolding
> that girdles the *trei ierarhi* monastery, wood and iron overlap and intertwine. "i'll
> > never turn the corner so long as
> her roundness, in my disc-jockey hands, plays the music of the spheres."
> "just the same way that rust and woodworms marry (with white bridal sails) till
> > kingdom come." "more than anything else,
> the saying *even if i don't have, I still give!* best suits her, when in my arms she takes
> > me between
> parentheses." "the same way that boys and girls form a circle, holding each other
> > around their shoulders/their waists, dancing the *hora*,
> with an embroidered girdle from the *trei ierarhi*."
>
> > > > > > > > ("(po)em in flesh and blood")

As the book's title suggests (not the sole element with this purpose), we do not deal here with mere poems, but with the poet as a human being, in flesh and blood. And that's how it is, for these emblematic *Canting Arms* aim to be a transcription of the poet himself, caught between biography and destiny, between happenstance and writing. All—literally all—is absorbed by Galaicu-Păun in his writing, including passion, love and lust, and the seen/lived either as reading or as writing. Reading and writing are rewritten, without emotional fever (never bodily), but only with a fever for symbols. This processing into symbol— or just raising into the symbolic—makes of his poetry an apotheosis of the real. No matter how grotesque it is, how repugnant or traumatic, poetry raises it to a symbolic valence. Galaicu-Păun's denunciations are, in fact, hymns, not necessarily, at first glance, of reality but of poetry's power of transfiguration. But once this power has been applied, once its effectiveness has been exercised, the reality that it attacks also transcends. It turns into hymns as traditional existential laments are raised to the symphonic register. Not for nothing does Munch's scream cross several poems, sometimes directly, other times only through echoes. The symphony of this scream has been written by Emilian Galaicu-Păun.

— Al. Cistelecan

On Emilian Galaicu-Păun

Emilian Galaicu-Păun is one of the leading European poets of today, not only in the Republic of Moldova and Romania but also, more broadly, across the continent. His poetry is metaphorically brilliant and audacious, neo-expressionist, firmly grounded in the concrete and the "real," as well as psychologically intense, satiric, always erotic or on the verge, and not infrequently wildly, if strangely and surprisingly, comic. His playful textualism is replete with allusions, cagy irony, puns ranging from flagrant to subtle, and religious, historical, political or cultural references, as well as personal narrative and echoes of oral tradition. At times the energy of his poetry seems barely constrained by the boundaries of his lines, but his instinct for form nonetheless keeps this abundance in check, lending a shapeliness in paradoxical tension with his luxuriant imagination.

In short, Emilian Galaicu-Păun has proven himself a gifted, indeed a major, contemporary voice, a master of the rich and varied stylistic strands of poetic tradition in the Romanian language, and his books add up to a widely respected and honored literary creation.

•

Emilian Galaicu-Păun, born in 1964 in Unchiteşti in what was then known as the Moldavian Soviet Socialist Republic, graduated in philology from the State University in Chişinău in 1986, then received a doctorate at the Maxim Gorky Institute of Literature, Moscow, in 1989. He is fluent in Russian and French in addition to Romanian, and phrases from these two languages pepper his poems, the French frequently erotic, the Russian vernacular and vulgar.

His numerous roles are impressive: poet, novelist, essayist, journalist, and editor-in-chief of the most notable publisher in Moldova, Cartier Publishing House, Chișinău. He has also been an active correspondent for Radio Free Europe, offering weekly programs on literature and commentary on East European/Moldovan politics, about which he also blogs.

Galaicu-Păun has published ten books of poetry, among them *Abece-Dor* [ABC-Desire] (Chișinău, 1989); *Cel bătut îl duce pe cel nebătut* [The Beaten Carries the Unbeaten] (Cluj-Napoca, Romania, 1994); *Yin Time* (Bucharest, 1999); a pair of volumes of selected poems, *Arme grăitoare* [Canting Arms] (Chișinău, 2009) and *A-Z.best* (Chișinău, 2012); and his first books of new poetry in a decade, *Apa.3D* and *A(II)Rh+eu* (Cartier, 2019)—these titles are puns, the second opaque and untranslatable in any direct way. *A-Z.best* is the textual basis of this English translation. At Galaicu-Păun's suggestion, this book bears the occult title he gave his 2009 book of selected poems, *Canting Arms*, a heraldic term denoting a polysemous escutcheon correlative to the poet's complex style.

Galaicu-Păun has been honored with numerous prizes in Moldova and Romania, including the title of Knight of the Order of Honor in Moldova and two years later the presidential Order of Cultural Merit in the Grade of Officer—or as Galaicu-Păun facetiously described it on the Cartier website, with a characteristic wit and insouciance, lieutenant of literature. In 2019, he was awarded the George Bacovia poetry prize in Romania. (He also received the 2005 Moldovan National Literature Prize, but returned it the following year because of the politics of the subsequent honoree.)

Emilian Galaicu-Păun's 2011 novel, *Țesut viu: 10 x 10* [*Living Tissue*], came out in English from Dalkey Archive Press in 2019; his work has been translated into more than twenty languages. He himself translates from French into Romanian, mainly histories and studies of Western symbology, including work by Robert Muchembled, Roland Barthes, and multiple books by Michel Pastoureau, but he has also translated a volume of Georg Trakl's poetry and Edward Lear's poem "The Scroobious Pip."

On the Translators

Adam J. Sorkin has translated more than seventy books of contemporary Romanian literature and has won a variety of international prizes, among them the Poetry Society (UK) Prize for Marin Sorescu's *The Bridge*, the Kenneth Rexroth prize in the U.S., the Ioan Flora and Poesis prizes in Romania, and honors from the Moldovan Writers' Union. For his translation activities he has been granted Fulbright, Rockefeller Foundation, Arts Council of England, New York State Arts Council, Academy of American Poets, Witter Bynner Foundation, Soros Foundation, Romanian Cultural Institute and NEA support.

Diana Manole is a Romanian-Canadian scholar and literary translator, as well as the author of nine collections of poems and plays. She holds a doctorate from the University of Toronto and since 2006 has been teaching theatre, literature, and creative writing at universities in Canada. She has also translated or co-translated seven poetry collections from/into Romanian and, with Adam Sorkin, earned 2nd prize in the 2018 John Dryden Translation Competition. *Canting Arms* is her fifth book translated in collaboration with Sorkin.

Lidia Vianu, a poet, novelist, critic, and translator, is Professor Emeritus of Modernist and Contemporary British Literature at the University of Bucharest, where she founded the MA Programme for Translation. She is also Director of the *Contemporary Literature Press* and has been Fulbright professor at UCal Berkeley and SUNY Binghamton. Vianu has written more than twenty books of literary criticism, among which are *The AfterMode, T.S. Eliot: An Author for All Seasons* and *Censorship in Romania. Canting Arms* is her ninth book in collaboration with Sorkin.

Claudia Serea is a Romanian-American Pushcart Prize winning poet with poems and translations featured in numbers of prominent literary journals. She has published seven poetry collections, most recently *In Those Years, No One Slept* (Broadstone Books, 2023).

Rareșa Galaicu, an Assistant of the EU High Level Adviser on Customs and Tax Policy, has over a decade of experience in translation and is a sworn interpreter/translator certified by the Ministry of Justice. She is the poet's daughter.

Cristina Cîrstea Danilov began her career with two books of poetry but went on to a career in psychology. She has published a volume of psychological essays and worked as a psychological counselor. Recently she has been writing on psychology for magazines and a daily newspaper.

Stefania Hirtopanu is a freelance translator and Romanian language teacher living in England. She has also translated Northern Irish poets into Romanian.